afterwork

An honest discussion
about the retirement lie
and how to live a future
worthy of dreams.

1) Think about 3 things you intend to do as a
result of this book. (Increase Work outs)

2) Increase Journaling

3) Calendaring

Joel Malick • Alex Lippert
with Dean Merrill

Contents

Introduction   1

Part One: Dreams and Disappointments

What Now?   5

You're Not a Portfolio, You're a Person   15

Part Two: Ten Keys to Consider

Key No. 1 — A Sense of Purpose   25

Key No. 2 — Calendar   41

Key No. 3 — Movement   49

Key No. 4 — Journaling   59

Key No. 5 — Faith   71

Key No. 6 — Learning   83

Key No. 7 — Awareness   93

Key No. 8 — Connection   107

Key No. 9 — Generosity   115

Key No. 10 — Awe   129

Part Three: Closing Thoughts

The Power of a Cornerstone Habit   143

Since We're All Terminal Anyway...   153

Introduction

In our line of work, we meet people every week who have saved and invested enough money to live comfortably for the rest of their life.

As they blow out the multitude of slow-burning candles on their birthday cake, they realize their relationship with time has changed. They no longer think in terms of "How old am I?" Instead their attention turns to "How many more years do I have?" Their thought process has changed from open possibility to a finite well that's running dry. When they think about life with all its memories, intricacies, pain, and joy, they begin to wonder, "Is this really all there is?"

If it's of value to you to live out your years ahead in the most purposeful and impactful way possible, this is the book for you. Who will you be *afterwork*?

PART ONE

Dreams and Disappointments

What Now?

Although for several years we'd known Carolyn,[1] a pleasant client of ours in her mid-fifties, we'd never met her husband, Bill. The day came when we finally sat down with the two of them. His graying hair bore testimony to his seniority — he'd just turned seventy — but he appeared to be in good health. His firm handshake and good eye contact let us know he wasn't shy.

Before we got down to business, one of us said in a friendly tone, "So, Bill, you've been retired for a couple of years?"

Out of the blue he volunteered, "Yes — and it's been the most challenging time of my life."

We had heard this kind of thing more than once from other recently retired clients. Somehow their dreams hadn't quite come true. In this case, we didn't want to put Bill on the spot; instead, one of us chose to ask about his previous job. Maybe this would yield some clues to his discomfort.

---

[1] Throughout this book's various stories, certain names, places, and other identifiers have been changed to respect privacy. However, the essence of each account is faithful to what occurred.

"I was the general manager of the big Ford dealership in Palo Alto for nineteen years," he explained. "I absolutely loved it. We had so many returning customers, because we did business the right way. We treated people with respect. It got to the point with a lot of these people that I didn't even have to negotiate on price, because they knew they were getting a fair deal."

"That's great," we responded. "The auto business doesn't always work that way."

"Yes, well, we created a different culture," Bill replied, warming to the subject. "I was determined to make this dealership a positive force in the community. Sure, it was hard work — ten to twelve hours a day, every day but Sunday. I lived on my feet, it seemed, meeting customers, managing staff. But I loved it." As Bill talked, he looked off into the distance as if to relive his past just one more time.

Carolyn, on the other hand, quietly nodded, saying nothing.

"So, what is your life like now?" we asked, turning the conversation to the present.

"Well, we've got this great property up in the Santa Cruz Mountains, about 2,300 feet elevation. It's a gorgeous area, and we absolutely love being outside the city. It's peaceful and quiet. We had a rustic mountain-style home built just the way we wanted. We even have some redwoods up behind our place."

But apparently this beautiful setting wasn't filling all the holes left by the transition. We waited.

"I spend the majority of my time maintaining this half-mile dirt road down to the highway," Bill continued. "I've got this little tractor that I fire up every time the rains wash away some of the roadbed. Gotta stay on top of the erosion. But in between times, when the sun is shining ..." He couldn't think how to finish the sentence. His demeanor, however, seemed to fairly ooze, *I guess I had my big season on the stage of life — and now it's gone.*

Not Unusual

In our work as financial advisors, we've heard this perplexity more than a few times. Once the conversation gets beyond the client's account balances and performance, strategy, the documents to be signed … and moves on toward *life satisfaction,* many people can turn out to be struggling. What are they supposed to do with all this "free time," they wonder?

How will they ever fill another fifteen or twenty years? It's almost as if they're asking themselves, *Who am I when I'm not "me" anymore?*

Bill is a lot more than a road maintainer. He's a leader, a doer, a dealmaker, a developer of other people's talents. While there's nothing wrong with Bill kicking back and enjoying a quiet view of the mountains or the ocean, this in itself cannot be his narrative for the future. He's got more than enough money to pay a company to come grade his road every couple of months — while he could go on engaging with people somehow. But what would that look like?

Our friend Dan Starishevsky, vice president and national speaker with the investment firm Jackson National, shared two graphs they constructed with data from the Bureau of Labor Statistics[2]:

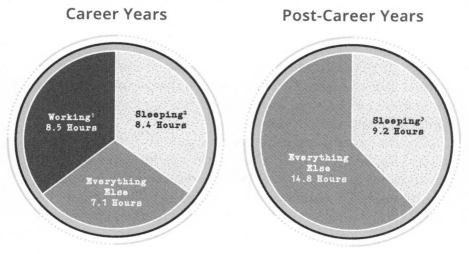

Career Years

Working[1]
8.5 Hours

Sleeping[2]
8.4 Hours

Everything Else
7.1 Hours

Post-Career Years

Sleeping[3]
9.2 Hours

Everything Else
14.8 Hours

Source: American Time Use Survey: 2019, published June 25, 2020; www.bls.gov/news.release/atus.nr0.htm
1 - Full-time employed person, average weekday hours worked   2 - Average employed American adult with children in the household
3 - Average non-employed American adult with no children in household

We are hard-wired to carry the burden of so many responsibilities — our busy careers, the wellbeing of our dependents (spouse, children), home upkeep, car maintenance, assisting our parents as they age, remembering birthdays and anniversaries, supporting various charities, keeping up with public issues, tax laws, social expectations … the list is long, and time is hardly enough.

Then comes that glorious, long-awaited day of retirement. All at once, the landscape lurches like an earthquake. "When we retire," says Starishevsky, "suddenly our free time more than doubles. We'll have around fifteen hours of time to fill every day…. Most people will say that sounds great! Can't wait. Sign me up!

"But the reality doesn't always line up with the daydream. What most people don't understand is that when we leave work, we leave a part of our identity behind — and that gap can't be filled with busywork.

"And these are supposed to be the 'golden years'? There has to be something more, right?"

> Vacations are wonderful because they're a counterbalance to working very hard. But how do you take a vacation when your whole life becomes a vacation?

If your plan for retirement is to "do nothing" because it sounds glorious today, the problem is that your entire life may come to feel like a void once you leave your career. And you can't fill a void with "nothing."

Vacations are wonderful because they're a counterbalance to working very hard, whether you're working in the traditional sense or working perhaps even harder to raise a family. You take a break from all the pressure and enjoy the beach. But how do you take a vacation when your whole life becomes a vacation? Suddenly the getaway loses its fulfillment.

People say that when they retire, "I'll finally get my time back." They don't realize that time can become their largest adversary once the post-career years start to unfold.

Let's Change the Vocabulary

Before we proceed any further, let's scrutinize the word *retire*. If we delve into a thesaurus, we will hit synonyms such as *recede ... withdraw ... retreat ... recall ... cease ... stop.* (The British have a quaint phrase, "become a pensioner.")

How great does all this sound? Is there anything exciting about these words? No.

The word *retire* carries an underlying connotation of something that's old, tired, worn out, not as useful as it used to be, even obsolete. It's fairly close to such clichés as "over the hill," "out to pasture," and "riding off into the sunset." Birthday cards for people above sixty-five often play on this stereotype with weak humor.

It's curious that when Dan Buettner, the Emmy-winning filmmaker and best-selling author, set out to research our planet's "blue zones" — where people are most likely to live to be 100, he found that ...

> In Okinawa they don't have a word for "retirement." They talk about *ikigai,* which means "why I wake up in the morning." People think of themselves as being useful into their 90s and even 100s. In Costa Rica the phrase is *plan de vida,* or life plan. In blue zones, the older you get, the more revered you are. It's not like "OK, Grandma, you've worked your whole life. Put your feet up." It's more like, "Grandma, we need you. We honor your decades of wisdom."[3]

In this book, we're going to try to sidestep the word *retire* in favor of more positive terms such as *your next season, the future, where you're headed,* and *the coming years.* This isn't meant to be just a word game. We truly believe you have decades of past professional, emotional, and personal experience worth drawing upon. As you come into the flexibility and freedom that your accumulated assets can float, you can put those powerful talents to great use for a wide array of people.

Beware the "Sugar Rush"

For the first ninety days or so, it seems downright blissful. The first Monday morning you don't have to deal with an alarm, you're euphoric. You can sleep in as long as you like. Tuesday morning, it's the same blessing. Wednesday … Thursday … Friday …. So far, so good.

You can putter around the house in your pajamas if you like. You can pull out that long-neglected list of home improvements and repairs. You can spruce up your lawn and cultivate your flower beds. You can go on an expensive vacation.

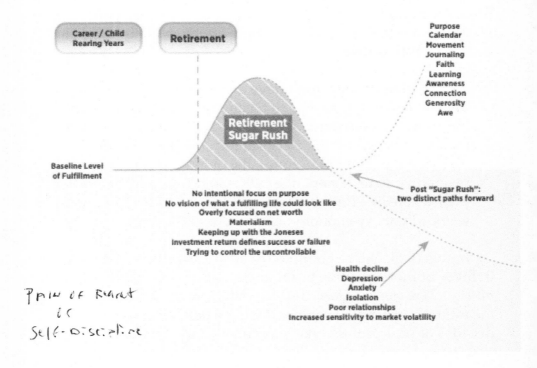

PAIN OF RMRT
iS
Self-Discipline

But before too many months go by, the sugar rush of retirement wears off, and then what? Here is an honest confession: We in the retirement planning industry have missed the most critical components of your future. Our focus and analyses have been far too narrow. We've allowed you to define success as a performance return number. We've made it seem as though you're on track if you hit your savings goals. We've swamped you with charts and graphs, research reports and corporate profiles, to the point of making you blurry. Along the way, we've failed to direct your focus to what matters more.

Honestly, what was the point in getting all the financial aspects right if in the end you don't even enjoy your life? This question deserves deep reflection.

Surprising News

I (Joel) was speaking to a convention group of about 200 people about this perspective, during which I said the following:

"You have value. (Notice, I didn't say "had." I said *"have."*)

"You have capability.

"You have wisdom.

"You have financial resources.

"You have time.

"You have experience.

"You've learned from many a mistake.

"You have persevered.

"This isn't your 'final chapter.' Instead, this can be your *greatest* chapter.

"Yes, it's probably the largest, most complex transition you will ever attempt in life. But you're not transitioning to a lesser version of yourself—just the opposite, if you choose. You're not a 'has-been.' You can absolutely become the strongest, most impactful version of 'you' imaginable. If you haven't given it much forethought till now, it's high time to do so."

I didn't think this was such a revolutionary concept at the time. But more than one person came up afterward to say, "I never thought of it that way! Thank you so much." I began to wonder if we were on to something here. It seemed to strike a deeper chord than I had anticipated.

The coming years can surpass any whimsical journey you had hoped for. This can be a graduation of sorts, a time of widening horizons and many options. You are still useful — to yourself, your family, your society, your world. Your potential influence can be astounding.

"Nothing to Do"?

The retirement lie is to think that a selfish retirement is a good one. It is a mistake to view the coming years as nothing more than cashing in on the money you've squirreled away, and hoping it doesn't run out before your death.

> " " The retirement lie is
> to think that a selfish
> retirement is a good one.

Most books you'll read on this subject will say something like "You've earned this; now here's how to make life all about you." But the truth is that you can be a lot happier than that — and a lot more fulfilled.

Our collaborator on this book, Dean Merrill, tells a humorous story about the afternoon on a trip when he and his wife were trying to get their two-year-old grandson to take a nap. In the hotel room where they were staying, they positioned the port-a-crib in one corner, lowered the window shades, gently put the boy down with his blanket, and retreated to the opposite corner. Soon began the admonitions that every parent and grandparent knows all too well.

"Reuben, close your eyes and go to sleep."

"Shhh, Reuben. No more talking."

"Stop wiggling around, Reuben. Just lie still."

The child would have none of it. Too much adrenaline was coursing through his veins.

After perhaps half an hour, Dean and his wife had to stifle their snickering when they heard the little tyke bemoaning his fate in the most mournful tone he could muster:

"Nothing to do ... nothing to do...."

More than a few retirees are muttering the same refrain these days, unfortunately. They stare out the window in the day, or at the ceiling at night, feeling untethered, useless, and bored. They wonder if they should have hung onto their previous position a few more years. Why go on living, if this is all the present can hold?

The respected Pew Research Center has found that the rate of "gray divorces" (in other words, break-ups for couples over the age of fifty) has doubled since 1990. Among those age sixty-five and older, the divorce rate has tripled in the same time period.[4]

A National Institutes of Health team crunched the numbers and concluded that "Depression and depressive symptoms are significantly associated with retirement in late middle-aged U.S. workers."[5]

It doesn't have to be this way. Answers are available — and most of them have nothing to do with dollar signs. The retirement riddle *can* be solved.

You're Not a Portfolio, You're a Person

Imagine that the grand evening of your retirement dinner has come at last. The food is exquisite, the ambience elegant throughout the room. Photos and displays of your career stand on easels nearby. Your boss, or perhaps the chairperson of your board, makes a glowing speech. Your loyal staff puts on a humorous sketch, or perhaps even a good-natured roast. Jokes are told, and everyone laughs heartily.

Eventually, your turn comes to stand and offer a few words. "Well, tonight I'm proud to say that, after twenty-eight years with this organization, I've amassed a retirement portfolio of $872,000. Now I get to start enjoying the hard-earned fruits of my long and demanding labors."

No. You'll not be saying any such thing—and not just because it would sound pompous and self-aggrandizing. You would instead speak about the warm relationships you've built, the new products or services launched by not just yourself but a whole team of people, the appreciative notes or reviews sent by customers and clients. You would thank your family members for their support through stressful times. You might even tell a story or two of how competitors showed their respect.

And you would be sure to include two or three guiding principles that held you steady along the winding road.

That is because you are a living, breathing human being whose social connections are foundational to your existence. You are not just a pile of money. You're a person. And next week, next month, next year after you leave the payroll, you will still be that person.

Getting Beyond the Numbers

I (Alex) have had many discussions with a client who has always been fixated on a net worth number. "If I can reach that amount one day," he would say, "then I can be free to do what I've always wanted to do." I finally asked him once, "Do you really think an extra comma and some zeroes are going to change anything in your life or who you are"? He paused, as if he'd been struck by lightning!

"What's my return?" is a common question we hear when we sit down with clients to review their portfolios. They want to hear a good number. But this is truly among the less important factors in building a post-career life. If you're a slave to the stock market (something completely illogical and emotionally driven in the short term), you will inevitably be tossed around like a plastic bag in a windstorm. Do you really think it reasonable to base your view on something so fickle and volatile?

Obviously, we believe in growing and compounding our clients' investments over the long term, to combat a number of risks and forces such as achieving a sustainable level of wealth based on spending, to stave off inflation, and to prepare for increasing healthcare costs as they age. We actually enjoy this delicate process. But whether you "beat the market" or outperform your loquacious neighbor across the fence is hardly relevant to what truly matters.

If you think your financial advisor exists solely to boost your returns, you're stuck in a 1980s broker-style model that is far short of why we come to work each day. The eminent novelist and poet Robert Louis Stevenson said it well: "Do not judge each day by the harvest you reap but by the seeds that you plant." What the market does today should never be the measure of your happiness or contentment. It's a huge waste of energy.

Sad to say, we literally have clients for whom the market dictates their mood for the day! If we happen to be meeting with them during a market downturn, they walk in with a furrowed brow and a heavy sigh. If the market is soaring, they're suddenly the nicest, most happy-go-lucky people you'd ever want to meet.

Actually, the human psyche seems to give more weight to negative things. The power of a loss is twice as great as the joy of a gain. When we tell people that, throughout history, the stock market has actually been up three out of four years, they can hardly believe us. *What?? No way!* Their assumptions are the opposite: three down years for every one good year. This has become their narrative.

Or they'll say, "Boy, the stock market sure is more volatile than it used to be." No, it's not. There's ample data to prove it.

We actually advised one worried client of ours to stop watching CNBC, Fox Business, and the other breathless minute-by-minute updates and analyses. She was reluctant at first; after all, she had tracked these indexes for years. But she finally took our counsel.

The result? She's no longer worried! "I don't even know if the financial news these days is good or bad," she admits. "I just come see you guys once a year, and you tell me how my portfolio is doing. I'm genuinely happier."

She is trusting us to do the monitoring, so she doesn't have to.

The Fear Factor

What's driving the angst in many intelligent, successful people is actually *fear,* whether they would admit it or not. Every four years, it seems, we hear the same refrain from clients: "Well, I better not make any changes—there's an election coming up." It's as if they're thinking, *If So-and-so wins the White House, that's it! The economy is doomed! We'll all fall off into the ocean!*

Another common pretext: "We're probably heading into another recession, aren't we? Should we liquidate our investments and just sit on cash for now?"

We work with one couple, both in their early sixties, who have a net worth of approximately $4 million ... but tell us every year how much they both hate their jobs. "We can't wait to retire!" they exclaim. "But not now. We'd lose our health insurance."

We have demonstrated to them in many different ways how they could easily stop working tomorrow and would face almost no possibility of running out of money, even if they tripled their spending and lived to be 102. They are as hedged and protected as a couple can be. They have children and grandkids—some locally, others out of state. When this loving pair pull out their phones to show us pictures, their eyes light up with pure joy. But they rarely see any of these family members face-to-face, unless during a preplanned get-together at Christmas or some other holiday.

Why are they so fearful? Well, there's "the next recession" and "the coming election"—plus they're not quite old enough to get Medicare. The truth is, with their nest egg, they could buy private health insurance and not even miss the money. So they continue to stay "busy" working long hours doing things they don't enjoy, storing up more accumulated funds than they know what to do with, while their clear passion (family, legacy) is slipping through their very capable fingers. *This is a travesty.*

"Fear is the mind-killer," science-fiction author Frank Herbert wrote in his famous work *Dune*. "Fear is the little-death that brings total obliteration." Fear manifests itself most often in stress, as people churn over the what-if's of their financial lives. They are locked in a dead-serious battle against the unknown, that ever-lengthening stretch of post-career years and even decades. Lifespans, after all, keep getting longer and longer, thanks to medical advances, improved standards of living, and other factors. Whereas in 1945 males in America could expect to live 63.6 years and females 67.9 years, today those numbers are much higher at 77.3 for males, 82 for females. The U.S. Census Bureau and National Center for Health Statistics (NCHS) project those figures to increase by approximately 6 years in length by 2060.[6]

> "Fear is the mind-killer. Fear is the little-death that brings total obliteration." –Frank Herbert

Some of the most persistent fears have to do with figments of the imagination. I (Joel) have a son who, despite all evidence, feels he has to get down on his hands and knees each evening and see if any monsters are lurking under his bed. If he doesn't check every night, he can't get to sleep. My wife and I have assured him a hundred times that our house is entirely safe and monster-free — it doesn't do any good.

Isn't it a shame when intelligent adults let fabricated fears put them in mental prison? President Franklin D. Roosevelt put it boldly in his first inaugural address (1933) amid the worst of the Great Depression, "Let me assert my firm belief that the only thing we have to fear is fear itself — nameless, unreasoning, unjustified terror which paralyzes needed efforts to convert retreat into advance."

From our experience, fear and anxiety manifest themselves in excuses to avoid making important decisions in many seasons of life, especially surrounding the future. Like our clients who wish dearly to retire and have the means to do so, their focus is diverted toward irrelevant factors. The root causes of their delay are the underlying fear of the unknown and the lack of mental preparation for their futures after work.

Many of us inadvertently choose the status quo, even if it's not fulfilling and in fact opposite of what we truly want, instead of stepping out bravely into a new and better life.

It reminds us of that ancient account of the Israelite people, who had been dramatically freed from slavery. But as soon as they hit a few challenges in the desert, they quickly wanted to exchange this freedom for more of their past and began whining to their leaders Moses and Aaron, "If only we had died by the Lord's hand in Egypt! There we sat around pots of meat and ate all the food we wanted, but you have brought us out into this desert to starve this entire assembly to death."[7] We all find comfort in the known; we get anxious when we encounter the unknown, whether it has a name or not.

A VUCA World

The acronym VUCA stands for "Volatile, Uncertain, Complex and Ambiguous". It was coined by a team of researchers at Harvard to explain the world that we live in. We naturally envision life and the world surrounding us as being orderly and logical whereas in reality, the world is far from it. There is a constant flow of crises and challenging-to-comprehend developments that are at odds with the tranquil and linear expectation we seem to hold in our minds of what the future holds. The truth is that we are in a permanent state of flux and uncertainty and so accepting the fact that the world is VUCA can help one realize how much is truly out of our control. This realization leads to a far more important understanding about what is actually in our control.

Control Only What You Can

The need is to be brave enough to embrace the future, understanding that it won't be easy, but it can be great. After all, how many true achievements that made us proud in our past life were easy? Not many. But the freedom of the Promised Land is still superior to the bondage of Pharaoh's chain gangs.

We need to focus on what we *can* control. We can't control the cyclical nature of investment markets, the timing of recessions, the rise and fall of corporate earnings, the unexpected tragedies near at hand or abroad. It makes no sense to obsess over these things.

Here are the things that everyone *can* control:
- Planning with phases in mind. (From age sixty to seventy-five, you'll probably spend more on airline tickets; after that, not so much—but more on health care.) It's wise to take the big-picture view.
- Healthy living
- Managing taxes
- Making sure wills and beneficiary designations are up to date
- Deciding where to live
- Uses of insurance
- Nurturing relationships
- Maintaining personal disciplines
- Controlling your reactions when adversity arises

And that is what this book is all about. We have to be intentional about our future. We can't just "let the chips fall where they may." Otherwise, we may end up like the character in Hemingway's *The Sun Also Rises,* who was asked, "How did you go bankrupt?" His reply: "Two ways. Gradually and then suddenly."

A lack of planning for the post-career season can lie dormant for years, until suddenly, "Oh, no! It's here!" None of us want to career into that predicament.

In the next section of this book we will delve into ten *nonfinancial* factors that can make a huge difference in your future. You may find that most are not easy. But we're not selling "easy." We earnestly want you to shape your future into what it can be by approaching this season of life fully aware and with intention.

The earlier you begin, the better the results. Just as you have accumulated financial assets over your lifetime, you can accumulate benefits over time through embracing these ten habits. Let's get busy moving you off the retirement lie and into your purpose.

PART TWO

Ten Keys to Consider

Key No. 1 — A Sense of Purpose

Little kids are infamous for pestering grown-ups with *why* questions. "Why are bananas yellow?" "Why do I have to take a nap?" "Why is the dog chasing his tail?"

But one of the biggest *why* questions that nags at our adult minds, especially as the years add up, is this: *Why am I here, anyway?* As we keep living, we want to do more than just pamper ourselves and "be happy."

There is a big difference between *happiness* and *meaningfulness*. Happiness is what we think we want. So we pursue it ... but the problem is, it's often just a pursuit of self. Ultimately it can end up thwarting true fulfillment. We realize later that it wasn't at all what we wanted, and now we've wasted a lot of our most irreplaceable resource, which is time.

Henry Ford once observed, "If I had asked people what they wanted, they would have said 'a faster horse.'" We today can behave almost as shortsightedly if we say, "If only I had that faster sports car, a better home, a beach getaway ... if only I didn't have to go to work anymore." We think these things will make us happy — and when they don't, we keep looking for yet more food to feed the happiness monster.

Something greater is at stake here. Meaningfulness is a different animal. It looks outward, not inward toward our surface-level self. It focuses on others — family, community, acquaintances, even strangers — whose lives we might serve and enrich.

Happiness is looking to *win* something. Meaningfulness is looking to *change* something for the better.

> ❝ Happiness is looking to win something. Meaningfulness is looking to change something for the better.

Yes, Thomas Jefferson put "the pursuit of happiness" into the Declaration of Independence as a fundamental American right. None of us would disagree. Without this basic right, we wouldn't have freedom. However, happiness is a lagging indicator; it's not some special circumstance that you find by directly looking for it. It's more organic than that. It blossoms out of one's purpose.

When we see our purpose as larger than ourselves, we can push past that pursuit toward meaningful fulfillment (which, in our opinion, is actually an underlying requirement for true happiness). Even when hardships arise — and they will — we will withstand them better. The boat called Happiness, on the other hand, takes on water in even the smallest of storms.

Peter Drucker, the famous management guru, was well into his nineties when he told an interviewer, "My definition of success changed a long time ago.... Making a difference in a few lives is a worthy goal. Having enabled a few people to do the things they want to do, that's really what I want to be remembered for."[8]

"Busy" Does Not Equal Purpose

Time and purpose can seem to be on a seesaw, always in opposition. When your schedule is jammed and you're short of time, you can assume that you're living a purposeful life.

But when you have too much time on your hands, purpose can seem to ebb, becoming a recognizable deficit for you. Back during the busy periods of your life, you didn't have time to reflect on whether your existence was meaningful; you were just trying to hang on and survive. But staying busy with an unending to-do list is not the same as living a purposeful life.

This applies just as much to the full-time homemaker as the business owner. Both can be swamped by their to-do lists. The clatter of daily life distracts them from the pursuit of purpose.

Richard Quinn, a compensation and benefits executive who retired in 2010, has written in a blog:

> Busy or bored? It's your choice. When I asked folks who were about to retire what they planned to do, typical answers included "play golf," "fish" and "tinker around the house." These aren't enough. But take heart: You'll soon be busy. The question is, will you be busy doing what you want to do?[9]

Your plan for the future must not just be to "stay busy in retirement." Lots of busy items have no tie to a purpose. You need to retire *to* something, not just *from* something. If you're not yet prepared to do this, you're not prepared.

Purpose Is Dynamic, Not Static

Before going any further, we need to say that a life purpose does not have to be cast in stone forevermore. It isn't a static thing. It is rather a process; it can run in seasons, during which you keep trying new things.

In other words, a sense of purpose is not a destination, a finished product you get in a chemistry lab when you mix the perfect amounts of right inputs into the glass flask. Purpose is rather a dynamic awareness of why you're getting up in the morning to accomplish something meaningful. That awareness may evolve over months or years — and that's all right.

Simon Sinek is a brilliant British-American author and motivational speaker who has appeared at everything from United Nations conferences to the Rand Corporation to the TEDx stage. We got to hear him at the 2018 Global Leadership Summit, where he spoke on "The Infinite Game." He said there are two games you can play in life, whether you're running a business, raising children, or even—you guessed it—heading into your post-career years.

The Finite Game (think basketball or football) has a set of fixed rules. Everybody knows how many players there are, how the clock runs, and how the score is tallied. At the end, there's a clear winner. Simon illustrated this by saying, "I spoke at an education summit for a world-famous tech company, and it seemed to me that most of the presenters spent most of their time talking about how to beat the other big tech company. I also spoke at an education conference at this second company, where 100 percent of the presenters spent 100 percent of their time talking about how to help teachers teach and learners learn. One organization was obsessed with beating their competition; the other was obsessed with where they were going."

In the Infinite Game, the goal is not to be the winner. There's no such thing as "best" or "first." There is only progress or lack thereof. Companies come and go, some do better than others, but there's no Finish Line where all the action stops and a winner gets crowned.

Yes, competition can be helpful if it pushes us all to be better than we were. But the point is not to beat somebody else. It is to be the best we can be.

> **❝❞ The point is not to beat somebody else. It is to be the best we can be.**

How does this relate to the post-career years? It means coming to understand that we're not playing a Finite Game.

Simon Sinek ended his speech that day with this: "Some people live their lives by the rules of the Finite Game. They wake up every day and get busy accumulating money and power. It's exhausting and stressful. At the end of life, they don't 'win.' They just die.

"In the Infinite Game, your true competition in life is yourself. Your objective each day is to become a better version of yourself. You have a cause to believe in. You live a service-oriented life. You push back daily against the human tendency to want to seek only self. Ultimately, your purpose is for others to say *they* are better because you were in their lives."

Do you find yourself naturally comparing yourself with others? Do you try to keep up with the Joneses? In fact, are you trying to *beat* the Joneses? If so, tell yourself once again that there's no trophy to win here. The only real "win" (if you need to use that term) is to leave things better than you found them. That may sound cliché, but your true fulfillment will come from the lessons you taught your grandkids, not the size of the trust fund you left them. Your fulfillment will come from the people who benefited from your generosity, not how many vacations you took or golf matches you played.

You don't "win" life; you simply have the opportunity to lead a life of meaning, and to pass that sense of meaning on to others. (Suggestion: You might even pass a copy of this book on to the Joneses, inviting them to join you in this journey of focusing on things that truly matter!)

If you're a Type A personality who has always striven to be Number 1 (professionally, even personally), you might stop and consider the fact that this is a self-defeating chase. How so? Because the moment you achieve this goal, the drive to keep growing and improving vanishes; there are no longer any benchmarks for you to beat. Soon the old saying "It's lonely at the top" comes into play — but for a different reason than is assumed. Most people use that saying to imply that the one at the top is constantly having to fend off wolves who want to supplant the leader. We employ the saying in a different way —

to show that the mindset of comparing ourselves to others leads to isolation. Whether you're in first place or last place, there's always room for improvement and growth.

It's Not All about You

Most retirement books, articles, and seminars portray this season of life as the time you can finally be selfish. They say things such as "You deserve ..." and "Imagine doing anything you want whenever you want to do it." The essence is that you've been working hard for the benefit of others (the company, your family members), and now it's finally *your* turn.

Wow, that's terrible advice!

We are not saying you shouldn't play tennis, swim, or go hiking. But what if instead of doing those things five times a week, you decided to mentor a needy person? What if you looked around for others (perhaps even in your own family) who are suffering silently? There's immense pain in every level of our society, and so much of it can be addressed with less selfishness and more benevolent action.

What if you played golf with a neighbor who's having a really hard time with a child who's ready to give up on their marriage of fifteen years because they think they're in love with someone else? Along with chopping up the fairways, you could be dissecting the interpersonal tensions in this troubled home and finding ways to ease them. How fulfilling would that be (even if you both scored way over par)? How momentous an effect could you have on everyone connected to that household (their children, for one)?

What if you connected with a distraught parent whose teenager is descending into the pit of drugs? You could bring up helpful resources — professional, medical, spiritual — that the parent may never have thought about employing.

All kinds of vistas open up when we start seeing that the post-career years are not *all about me*.

Terry Bromberg, a highly successful publishing and marketer in Los Angeles, was very good at what he did, "but it was about making a quarterly number," he says. "I made money and all that, but there wasn't a real passion there. When our daughter was about to graduate from high school, I realized that after so many years helping her with homework, there was now a void in my life. People have always told me that I'm a good teacher, and I've always felt somewhat of a kinship to the underdog."

As a result, Bromberg now spends volunteer time teaching math to high-risk youth and former gang members full of tattoos, as part of an organization called Homeboy Industries. Does he enjoy it? "There are days when I'm teaching, and it feels as though I'm almost having an out-of-body experience," he says. "I'm sitting over here watching me and I like what I see. It's very fulfilling when you see someone get their GED and driver's license and stay clean and want to be an accountant or something like that.

"Sure, we do classroom work, but we also talk about life. Somewhere down deep, they're probably thinking, 'I don't know why that guy cares about me, because few people in my life have—but he does.'"[10]

Isn't it interesting how, for decades in the past, people met you and asked, "So what do you do?"—but now the question shifts to "So what did you used to do?" This fits with the cultural motif of retirement as a world of *has-been*. Maybe they go on to ask a second question: "How do you fill your time now?"

Stunning. Before, you were a *doer of something*—but now you're a *filler of time!* Who wrote *that* script?

If you find yourself trying to fill time, you're definitely off course. How about changing the narrative? How about defining yourself without linking to a job, a position, a corporate identity. How about mapping out a fresh new purpose? Even if you're not retired yet!

Otherwise, you may wind up (once the brief sugar high of retirement wears off) back searching the job postings and updating your resume for a position you don't actually want. More than 25 percent of retirees do this! They are so uneasy that they want to run back to the familiar setting of the office or other job site. Economists have coined a term for this U-turn: "unretirement."[11]

Granted, some people go back into the work force because they truly enjoy it and have talents to keep offering. Others simply need the money. But a large group do this out of a sense of lostness, boredom, almost bereavement for what once was but is no more.

For all of us, the workplace structure played a huge role in defining our lives. The employer required certain performances from us, at certain times, with certain measurables, resulting in certain rewards (financial but also social). When that structure comes to an end ... then what? We were hardly aware of its place in our self-definition. Now, what is life going to be like without the structure? What will be our identity after we empty our desk space into a little box and carry home that old plant that somehow survived the fluorescent lights all those years? Who will we be then?

Where to Start

If this whole purpose thing seems hazy and nebulous to you, here are some questions to get you started: *"For what are you grateful?"* As you survey your situation in life, what makes you thankful? The answers for each of us actually represent a subconscious, inherent valuation. What we truly value is usually what we feel blessed in having.

And these blessings are most often *intangible.* Family. Health. Being surrounded by good souls. The quality education we received. Enough earnings to cover the basic necessities of life. (Beware, however, of limiting your list to just the financial, as in "I'm grateful I can afford to fly to the Mazatlan beach every January." Surely your blessings are more significant than that.)

If you have trouble getting started with this list, think about what vivid memories you hold from the past ten years. What were the highlight days of your work? Now go on to ask why those moments were significant. Soon you'll be finding genuine appreciation for their meaning.

True gratitude bypasses the material items of our existence to get down to what our hearts cherish. These things spark an inner joy, a nearly unexplainable sensation that we are fulfilled as we experience them. We all have moments of interacting with someone who gives us a simple smile or thank-you for investing in their life — and we get goosebumps inside. This kind of feeling is closely linked to a genuine *purpose* for our being alive. We want more of this fulfillment, whether we get paid for it or not. We ask ourselves how we can better the lives of those we cherish most. How can we leave a lasting legacy? (By the way, *legacy* and *financial inheritance* are not at all the same thing.)

From this list of things that make you grateful, you can then move on to ask, *"How might I pour more of myself into these things?"*

Take the example of family. No doubt your kids and grandkids are endlessly busy with school, sports, trips, and extracurricular activities, to the point that you almost can't find a way to shoehorn yourself in. Yes, you all get together for birthdays and Christmas, but is that the best you can do? Why does a formal date have to be locked on everybody's busy calendar for anything good to happen?

The grandparent can get around this problem by volunteering to drive the grandchild to school a day or two a week. Car time is great conversation time. Maybe the grandparent can get involved in coaching, or showing how to make something in the wood shop, or kitchen. What kid doesn't like to produce a yummy treat? If the goal is to enrich the life of a young person, don't let the formality of appointment-setting get in the way; be intentional and creative around the edges.

Ask yourself how you can offer your time, experience, expertise, or simply your willingness to make an impact on someone you care about (whether family member or not). Your unique strengths are meant to be used in this life. Many people are all around you whose life trajectories can be changed for the better if only you apply the tools you've spent a lifetime honing.

Your purpose does not have to be some innovative mega-project that brings you fame. It can be simple, even ordinary. But if it helps another person, and it brings you joy, it's worth pursuing.

Consider the little honeybee. Without purpose, the honeybee would lazily sit around not pollinating anything — which would be dreadful for our food supply. Did you know that 84 percent of all crops grown for human consumption need insects to pollinate them? Some crops, such as blueberries, cherries, and almonds, depend solely on honeybees; without them, the grocery shelves would be bare of these delights. The California almond industry pays for approximately 1.8 million colonies of honeybees annually in order to pollinate its 1 million acres of almond orchards.

The ecosystem is finely orchestrated for purpose. But what about mankind as a whole? How sad that multiplied thousands of people retire not only from their careers but also from their contributions to others, thereby depriving the society in the process.

Who is waiting for your "pollination"? Who can thrive only as you touch their life? To quote the estimable novelist Charles Dickens, "No one is useless in this world who lightens the burdens of others."

A third question is more personal: *"What am I passionate about? What gets my heart racing?"* This is highly individual, of course. You are a unique person, viewing the world through a personal set of eyes.

But now, once the necessity of paycheck is removed from the equation, what would you love to spend your days doing?

Your answers may or may not be the same as your spouse's — and that's okay. While common interests in a marriage are valuable, it's also fine to develop individual pursuits. Ask yourself, "What parts of my career did I really enjoy? Can I keep doing these things in an altered format? Is there a local organization that needs my expertise?"

We have a client named Paul who is great at crafting marketing messages. He found a local nonprofit that was doing great work but not telling its story very convincingly. Now he has some fun projects to do. He's helping the organization present itself more compellingly, and he's loving every minute of it.

Is there something you've always wanted to learn but never had the chance? Maybe you can take a course at a local university. Whether you get an A or not is beside the point. The point is to expand your horizon, engage in lifelong learning, and stretch your mind in a new direction.

With all our formats and systems in the business world, we sometimes forget the power of a personal passion. We know a pastor in Fort Collins, Colorado, who stepped out of a well-paying executive role to start an outreach to broken people: the addicted, the victimized, those with criminal records. His new church, called the Genesis Project ("place of new beginnings"), is swarming with ex-cons, biker dudes, women who have escaped the sex trade, you-name-it. In his book, he writes: "When I talk about the work these days, I sometimes get frustrated when I choke up. But I've never been happier in my life, and neither has Joy [his wife]. I told her long ago, 'I simply have to be part of something that makes me cry when I talk about it.'"[12]

Start in the Center

All this talk about purpose may strike you as a bit vague. Is it really all that important? Can't you just head into retirement and "play it by ear"?

Actually, that's not a good idea. Purpose is central. If life were the solar system, purpose would be the sun, around which all the planets revolve. Did you know that it would take 1,300,000 earths to fill up the sun's volume? In fact, the sun is 99.8 percent of the solar system's entire mass.[13] Without the sun, everything else would fly off into the void.

Without purpose, the rest of your life has no point of reference, no gravity. Yes, there are other important components of your solar system, such as the next nine keys we're going to cover in this book. But each of them, when implemented, orbits around your purpose.

As you start to articulate your sense of purpose, begin with what's most central. To give you a different analogy: Imagine that you're building a new home. Where does this start?

Well, your new home definitely needs a solid foundation. It's also going to need load-bearing walls. Early on, you're going to need electrical conduits to enable lights and appliances, and duct work to convey cool air in the summer and heat in the winter. None of these things is very exciting. But they set up the more glamorous features to be added later.

If life purpose is to be your house, the starting point is not the pictures you're going to hang on the wall, or that trip to Italy for your fiftieth anniversary, or that monthly game night with your old high-school friends, or those weekends of camping in the mountains. These will all be wonderful in due time. But first of all, you need a foundation, and framing, and drywall on which to hang these decorations. You have to first build the new structure before you can walk into it and start enjoying the pretty stuff.

That's the reason for a post-career purpose.

The money you've accumulated to fund this season of life is nothing more than raw lumber that will enable you to build your purpose. Earlier in your working life, you may have been too busy, or too financially strapped, to even contemplate this coming season. But now, it's a different story.

> **" " The money you've accumulated to fund this season of life is nothing more than raw lumber that will enable you to build your purpose.**

So carve out an hour in the early morning to reflect on what your purpose should be going forward. Or find a few quiet minutes each night before bedtime to "draw the blueprints" for what you want your "house" to be. If you're a person who believes in God, ask him for direction at this stage—and listen for any insights he might send your way. You want to glean all the wisdom and foresight you can, right?

In this book, we're not going to give you a set of architectural sketches to copy. You take the lead here, according to your unique personality and passions. Having asked the questions we listed earlier in this chapter, you can now start writing your own purpose statements. Yes, it would be good for you to commit these to actual text (on paper or a screen), where you can see them. (You can go back tomorrow or the next week or next month to revise and improve them; that's fine.)

Take up the challenge of framing your purpose for the future. Over the past years of your working life, you've no doubt been given more than one job description; if you were in management, you've drafted these documents for your subordinates. Now ... write *your own* job description for the coming years. Spell out the major values, activities, and outcomes. Let this become your North Star for the future.

Two Warnings

As you start to live out the sense of purpose you've written for yourself, let us mention a couple of sobering realities:

The first is, *prepare yourself for hardship.* There will be unpleasant surprises. Things won't always run smoothly. Life won't roll out the red carpet for you at every turn.

Rasmus Ankersen, a Danish entrepreneur and student of high-performance culture, tells about going to visit the MVP Track and Field Club in Kingston, Jamaica. As every sports fan knows, the Jamaicans are incredible sprinters all across world competitions. The coach at this club, Stephen Francis, agreed to show Ankersen around, telling him to show up for the 6:00 a.m. practice.

Ankersen arrived early, at 5:30, looking for a state-of-the-art training facility. Instead, he found himself staring at a worn-out field and shabby gymnasium. Had he gotten the directions wrong?

No, Stephen Francis soon appeared to explain that, while he strives to provide athletes with what they need, he also asks something of them in return. "I want an environment that tests people," he said, "and gives me the answer to what I believe is the most important question: Who wants it most? This place is not designed for comfort but for hard work. If you're driven by comfort and glamour, you won't want to come here. But if you really want to improve—to do better today than you did yesterday—then this club is the place to be."

One of his success stories is Asafa Powell. No American college had come to scout him during high school or offer a scholarship, despite Jamaica's reputation for fast runners. Powell, at six feet three inches and weighing 194 pounds, is too bulky to be a sprinter. But when Stephen Francis decided to work with him anyway, he searched the island until he found a 100-meter stretch of roadway with a steep *10-percent grade.* (Rarely do you find an American highway with more than a 5- or 6-percent grade.) Francis put him to work on this brutal slope. Well … that may have something to do with the fact that the adult Asafa Powell has gone on to break the 10-second barrier *ninety-seven times* in this race. He won a gold medal at the 2016 Olympics in Rio as part of the Jamaican 4 x

100-meter relay team. He also holds the world record for the 100-*yard* dash at 9.09 seconds.

Stephen Francis has one ruling principle that can be applied to any of us: *Hunger is more important than skill.* If you tell yourself you're just a normal person who probably isn't going to make much of an impact in the coming years, you probably won't. But if you're hungry to live a purpose-filled life, you can do it. It all comes down to hunger … desire … or to use an even stronger term, *grit* – the grit to forgo making everything comfortable as you get busy pursuing impact, day in and day out.

You don't have to be an exceptional talent with a lengthy resume of past achievement. You don't need to hope for "the breaks" along life's future path. You simply need grit.

Our second warning is this: *Beware of "retirement drift."* Our lives are always in danger of drifting from our spiritual or moral or performance standards. We slack off on hitting the gym as much as we should. We get distracted with other, more pleasurable pursuits.

The best-laid purpose plan for the future is vulnerable to drift over time. The ancient Chinese philosopher Lao Tzu warned us in his clever saying, "If you do not change direction, you may end up where you were heading." Is that really what we want?

Have you ever tried to lay down a line of orange cones for a youth soccer game in the park? You walk forward, dropping one cone after another in what you're sure is a straight line … until you get to the corner of the playing field. You turn around to admire your work, and sure enough, the line is crooked! *How did that happen?* you ask yourself. *I'm sure I walked straight!*

If on the next try, you were to turn around and walk backwards so you could see the cones you've already laid, your line would probably be straighter. But it might still be angling off in an unwanted direction.

C. S. Lewis wrote:

> Progress means getting nearer to the place you want to be. And if you have taken a wrong turn, then to go forward does not get you any nearer.
>
> If you are on the wrong road, progress means doing an about-turn and walking back to the right road; and in that case the man who turns back soonest is the most progressive man.[14]

What every soccer dad or mom needs is a plumb line—a tree or a post at the edge of the field to aim toward. It won't move. As long as you keep heading for that marker, your line of cones will be accurate.

If you set your course for the coming years according to a clear purpose, and muster the grit to pursue it daily come what may, you will achieve your goal of meaningfulness. Your life will count for something valuable. And you'll be happy with the result.

How will you set your purpose course?

In the previous chapter, we spoke about *what* to do in the days and months and years ahead — activities that are purposeful and meaningful, not just time-fillers.

In this chapter, we turn to the question of *when* to do those things.

Life up to now has been filled to the brim with structure, both at work and in the child-raising years at home. We've been telling ourselves, *Okay, I need to get up at 5:45 every morning in order to _____ before I head out the door.* Once at our place of employment, we've loaded up our calendars with weekly meetings, deadlines, and travel. Back home again, the kids have needed to be fed, to do their homework, and to get to bed at a certain hour. This has been our life, year after year. With only a certain number of available hours, we've had to constantly plan ahead and prioritize.

But once you "retire," most of the structure vanishes. You can sleep in as late as you want. Meetings in the conference room — who cares?! As we said in the first chapter, you have twice as many waking hours to use as you wish.

Some people think it's silly to keep a calendar now, because they have complete freedom to do — or not do — anything.

What does *not* change for most of us, however, is the inner drive to stay organized. If we somehow feel disorganized, a sense of stress begins to well up inside. Have you ever walked into a friend's or relative's cluttered garage or messy storage room, or even pantry, and started to feel queasy? Tools and boxes are lying haphazardly everywhere you look. If you wanted to find a simple screwdriver, or a can of mushrooms, you'd hardly know where to start. *Wow, how can someone live like this?* you murmur to yourself.

Well … what if someone could track your post-career life for a week? What would they see? Would it be disorganized and random? Would cobwebs be forming in important areas?

Manage Your Calendar

Time (like money) can greatly benefit us if we *manage* it. The details now will be different from the past, of course. Even the format (physical or digital) may be different. But the value of a calendar remains high. It makes sure we don't miss the fulfillment of a coffee shop date with our spouse, an afternoon hike, a volunteer stint at a church or other nonprofit, a play time with youngsters.

Yes, it allows for spontaneity. You can always change what you had planned previously. But if there's no base from which to begin, your whole life becomes a tangle of loose ends.

The point is *not* to fill every box, every hour with busyness. That is as much of a trap as not managing the calendar at all. If you fill your days with unending "noise" that isn't aligned to your purpose, you will miss the mark. Some people sit on an organization's board for no better reason than "that's what retirees do," rather than being committed to the mission and giving valuable input. And if you're a list-maker, you may feel good momentarily that you checked off all the items on your list for a given day or week or month. But what did it all mean in terms of your personal purpose?

> **❝❝** The point is not to fill every box, every hour with busyness. That is as much of a trap as not managing the calendar at all.

Some people are in the groove of writing a new to-do list every few days, copying over the unchecked items from the previous list so they'll be sure not to miss anything. A few souls are so compulsive they actually transfer previously *completed* tasks to the new list, just for the thrill of crossing them off again!

But if the task is hollow, this self-congratulation wears thin. Sooner or later, the *why* of the activity must be confronted.

Activity definitely has its benefits. Dr. Sheldon Cohen, psychologist at Carnegie Mellon University, and a grad student of his did a study of older adults who had volunteered at least 200 hours over the prior year. They found greater increases in psychological well-being—and even lower blood pressure!—than among non-volunteers. "Even commuting to volunteer sites and activities," they wrote in the journal *Psychology and Aging,* "may also increase physical activity, therefore decreasing hypertension risk."[15]

But the activity has to be planned, scheduled, and controlled. In our practice, we have some go-getter clients who stay so active they are hard to schedule for even a one-hour annual financial review in our office. "I'm too busy," they protest. They are so afraid of waking up some morning with nothing to do that they've packed their days and weeks with one activity after another, nonstop.

That's not *managing* a calendar. The goal is to strike a balance among service, rest, reflection, new experiences, disciplines, and connection. It is to structure your week or day in advance so you move forward intentionally, not just waking up each day to play life "by ear."

A different client of ours has the right idea, we think, by blocking some time every Tuesday to go to his adult kids' houses and simply fix things they haven't gotten around to — or don't know how to fix. What a great service to busy parents working fulltime and raising kids.

But this client also has established times to read, to do art, and to write. His structured, well-thought-out calendar helps him tremendously in his effort to remain on the path of purpose.

We heard about one pastor who made sermon preparation such a priority that, when cornered after church by someone wanting to see him on, say, Wednesday morning, would pull out his pocket calendar, take a quick look, and then reply, "Oh, I'm sorry — I have an appointment that morning. I'll be glad to see you a different time, though." The parishioner never knew that the pastor's pre-scheduled Wednesday "appointment" was with the writings of the prophet Isaiah or the apostle Paul! His managed calendar was keeping him on track in that moment, protecting his calling.

Mornings Are Strategic

A good calendar must begin with silencing the negative voices and worries that can often flood in after waking up and thinking about the upcoming day's realities. Your day needs to be kick-started to gain traction. Here are four items that belong up front. Try to engage at least two of them each day, moving among the four throughout each week:

- Physical movement (we'll unpack this in the next chapter)
- Spiritual growth
- Journaling (that's coming in a later chapter, too)
- Reading or listening to something inspirational or creative

All of these contribute to serious momentum and silence the voices that tell you you're tired, you're not good enough anymore, and what's the point anyway.

The rest of your morning should then be structured to manage your *energy* as well as your *time*. When are you the sharpest, most creative, most energized? For most people, the answer is morning. You can do more critical and creative thinking earlier in the day. This is "prime time."

A long-forgotten sage once observed, "Each season of life has its unique shortage. For the first twenty-five years of your life, your shortage is *money*. For the next twenty-five years of life, you hopefully have more money — but now you're short of *time*. And then you get to the third twenty-five years of life, when you have adequate money and definitely more time — but the shortage instead is *energy*."

If that's true, you need to maximize the output of what energy you still have. If one of your goals is to learn more about a certain period of American history, morning is the time to engage with this material. If you happen to love art and want to create illustrations for children, this is the time to get to your easel or sketch pad. If you've volunteered to write a strategic policy paper for the nonprofit where you volunteer, this is the time to get busy at your computer. Not only will you be more efficient at completing your meaningful aims, but you'll also feel better later in the day knowing you already did some heavy lifting.

What you do *not* want to do when you get up in the morning is hop onto Facebook, or scan emails, or see how the stock market is doing, or settle down to surf the TV channels! The very *last* thing you need is for Wall Street or Washington, D.C., to tell you how to feel today.

> ❝ What you do not want to do when you get up in the morning is hop onto Facebook, or scan emails, or see how the stock market is doing, or settle down to surf the TV channels!

Don't burn energy on things you can't control. They will color your thoughts for the rest of the day, keeping you from applying valuable time and energy on something that actually matters and will make a difference.

Do you have items in your calendar that you can profitably delegate to others? Financial concerns are one of these; that's why you have professional advisors, right? It is our job to monitor all the market ups and downs, so you don't have to.

We're not saying you should stick your head in the sand and ignore what's going on in the world. But don't give the gathering of news information a place in "prime time." Treat it like you treat lawn mowing or car maintenance: something to get to later in the day, when your focus and energy have already been applied to purposeful endeavors.

If you want an outline for a well-designed day, here's our recommendation:

- First, kick-start your momentum (see list on page 44).
- Second, create something; learn something; think through an important challenge.
- After lunch, get some of the mundane chores off your list.
- As evening comes, prepare for a meaningful connection with family or friends over dinner.

This isn't rocket science by any means, but it gives you tremendous advantage as you pursue your purpose day after day.

Are we ruling out a "lazy morning" once in a while? Not at all; those are fun. But if you have seven lazy mornings in a row, they just turn into ... mornings. Something can be "lazy" only in contrast to "non-lazy." And in the end, that's what you want.

Seasons and Texture

On a broader scale: The post-career life can greatly benefit from our being aware of its seasons — periods of months that are different from what came before, or will come in the future.

If you live in a climate that has four distinguishable seasons, you know that spring has a certain texture or flavor, summer is different, fall is another kind of season, and certainly winter (which may or may not be your favorite) has its uniquenesses. Some things you do outside in the warm summertime … others fit better in winter.

If your life doesn't have seasons, then you don't have markers — moments in your consciousness when you take stock, noting accomplishments, progress, and fulfillment. You need times to look at yourself and say, *I accomplished this, and I'm proud of it. Now I'm going to turn my attention to* _____. Calendar is a way of marking ebb and flow to your day, your week, your year, your life. It's about structuring themes and seasons that create fulfillment. A calendar helps you assess whether the many parts and pieces are actually aligning with your goals and priorities.

Vacations are especially valuable for taking note of the larger picture. You get out of your normal setting and see things you missed along the way. You see what brought you joy, and what was a sidetrack. You start making plans for what will be different and better once you get back home again.

And you remind yourself that you don't need to be busy all the time. You can embrace silence. It could actually be useful to set aside certain times for that. If you don't, you'll find that the idea of quiet reflection never quite seems to happen.

Give yourself permission to sit quietly. Life was never meant to be slavery to the to-do list. Let your calendar reflect the best version of you, the fulfillment of what you believe you're called to do in this most wonderful season of your life.

Key No. 3 — Movement

When we sit down with a client, the first topic is not normally the hard numbers of their portfolio or strategy. We ask how they're doing in general, what's new in their life, and often about their last fun travel experience.

Dave and Barb were glad to tell us about their recent excursion to Europe with their kids and some of the grandkids. It wasn't cheap, but they'd saved for it along the way. This had been a goal of theirs; they'd always preferred to spend their assets on experiences as opposed to things. As they described the trip, we could see them both light up.

However, when the conversation turned to the next year, it became apparent that they were coming to grips with the fact that the Europe trip may have been the last one — not because of finances, but because of their physical health. They admitted they didn't feel strong enough to attempt a trip like that again.

Now of course, as we all age, medical issues start to keep us from doing certain things we would like to keep doing. We don't need to feel bad if we simply can't engage in as much movement as we'd like. But the fact of the matter is that Dave and Barb could have been more active over the last decade to keep themselves in much better physical shape, and they chose not to. Now to live an active life seemed like an impossible hill to climb. It begs the question: How many future trips and memories with family were they forfeiting?

It's All Relative

If you're getting uneasy now with this chapter's topic, please relax. Hear this important statement: *Exercise or movement is a completely relative undertaking.* We're not going to browbeat you into becoming an ultra-marathoner. Put out of your mind any image of Forrest Gump running back and forth across America for three years!

Something as simple as a brisk walk through the neighborhood can start to produce remarkable results in your life. Whatever your health or circumstance, you can benefit from a more active, movement-filled existence.

The point is not for you to out-perform somebody else you know or have seen on television. The point is to slowly, gradually increase your own capacity for a healthy existence, to be a little stronger in six months or a year than you are today.

This stage of life comes with certain aches and pains you fortunately didn't have to navigate earlier in your life. That's no excuse not to find something that works for you. I (Joel) am extremely proud of my mom, who deals with incredible sciatic pain in her lower back and legs. A great client and physician I know suggested that she find a good sitting bike, because walking is unbearable, and it's important for body and mind to keep things moving. She now has the bike set up in her back patio and loves the daily routine and quiet time that comes from the exercise — which also happens to help her pain. We do what we can with what we have.

The Odd Road Forward

The next statement may sound contradictory, but it's true: *Discomfort creates comfort.* What we mean by that is what you foresee as being uncomfortable or challenging is in fact worthwhile. When discomfort stems from challenging yourself in new ways, it actually creates comfort long-term. Thus, the way to experience true comfort is to be "comfortable" in being uncomfortable.

> ❝ Thus, the way to experience true comfort is to be "comfortable" in being uncomfortable.

Exercise is a perfect example of this inverse relationship. It's always uncomfortable. Your heart beats faster than your resting heart rate, your lungs are forced to come alive under the exertion, your pores sweat, muscles start to burn ... you're definitely uncomfortable. But how does it feel when you finish exercising? You're glad to be done for the day. A few days or weeks later, you start to notice that stairs are slightly less burdensome. Lifting grocery bags or suitcases is a little less strenuous. You find yourself able to be on your feet longer.

Subconsciously, your body benchmarks itself against its prior self and shows you how far you have progressed, even if your shell hasn't seemed to change much. These small victories over time are enormously meaningful to your mental confidence and self-worth. This slow but noticeable progression gives some of the strongest benefits of exercise and movement in one's life.

We all need personal victories—something to be internally proud of. Getting up on our feet and more active is a way to chalk up small victories. If you start with five-minute walks ... and later in the year you're walking a mile or two and feeling great ... that progression will bring a smile within you. It is real success, not bound to societal or cultural biases, but simply because it's *you*, and you know you have improved. You feel better, and remember all the steps it took to reach that new lofty point.

Then a year later, perhaps you are slowly jogging a bit. Each milestone becomes a challenging summit to reach, and feel good about. The first summit begets the next, and so on. You keep telling yourself, *I'm getting better, I'm doing well. I'm becoming healthier. I can do more activities with my children, grandchildren, and friends.*

People wonder how someone could ever run a marathon or even a longer race. It is the culmination of this ongoing progression of battling oneself and continuing to challenge what they previously believed to be impossible. As they continue to do that, they eventually wake up one morning and decide to go on a long run before breakfast.

For each of us, the small victories we achieve by being active are an example of the right type of victories. Benchmarking ourselves against our former selves, as opposed to comparing ourselves to others, is the path to real fulfillment. Laying aside the relentless pressure to compare ourselves to others is the only way to progress and to feel true accomplishment. As Simon Sinek cleverly states in his book, "Better is better than best." What he means by that is, you're not doing this to be "the best," so just relax. You're not trying to win the award for "Most Strenuous Senior Worker-Outer." You don't need to run more miles than Pat, or show up earlier than Doug. This is a battle to become a better *you*.

A Cornerstone Habit

The more you move, the more you start to notice effects on other parts of your life. Your blood pressure drops, you are less stressed, you find yourself to be less anxious about life, you have time for self-reflection, and you can better your relationships because you are more grounded.

Thus, exercise becomes a cornerstone for solidifying many other things in your life. You feel a sense of accomplishment on many fronts. You go through a whole winter without getting bogged down by common colds and other sicknesses. Perhaps you'll even visit your doctor less often, and spend less at the pharmacy!

A scholarly study says:

> The beneficial effects of regular physical activity on health are indisputable in the field of modern medicine.... According to a US Department of Health and Human Services report on physical activity, regular exercise significantly reduced causes of mortality by up to 30 percent for men and women. These health benefits are seen consistently across all age groups and racial/ethnic categories....
>
> In addition ... regular exercise ... lowers prevalence of chronic disease(s).... Individuals who exercise regularly exhibit slower rates of age-related memory and cognitive decline in comparison to those who are more sedentary.[16]

Who would have guessed that working your arms and legs would do battle against Alzheimer's in your brain?

Maybe you already knew that. But there's more....

Being in the Now

Movement and exercise helps you step away, albeit briefly, from the status quo, the proverbial "grind" of life. Even if you walk the same exact route and wear the same jacket and shoes, movement is never redundant. Each day is unique, and your thoughts, circumstances, and body are always changing. So each time you get on your feet and move, it's a new experience.

Physical movement takes your thoughts away from the busyness of life and helps you be in the moment, the "now." This is a much researched and followed practice; in fact it's a chief underlying theme of mindfulness. Being in this exact moment helps clear your mind of the never-ending clutter of to-do lists as well as useless emotions and non-beneficial self-speak. It helps you experience life to the fullest in this very second.

We are aware that many runners listen to music on their runs, to distract their minds from the discomforts of their breathing and sweating. But in so doing, they miss this "nowness" of the activity. The next time you exercise, try to have no stimuli besides your own mind. Really focus on the now. After some practice, you may find more comfort within that space than you ever thought possible. Drop the music and other distractions.

> **Physical movement takes your thoughts away from the busyness of life and helps you be in the moment, the "now."**

At first, you will notice that your brain barrages you with thoughts. (If you don't believe this, stop what you are doing right now, lay down this book, and sit quietly for five minutes. Don't focus on any specific thought that knocks at your mental door. Just "be.")

Not living in the now is undoubtedly one of the reasons why time seems to pass too quickly in life. If we constantly focus on the future, then when the future arrives, our new focal point will once again be on the future, without much regard to the present second, the present breath we are inhaling. Have you ever been at a family gathering where a main topic of discussion was about setting the date and place for the *next* family gathering or upcoming plans with family members?

A Harvard Medical School publication carries the unusual title "Exercising to Relax." It says in part:

Aerobic exercise is key for your head, just as it is for your heart. You may not agree at first; indeed, the first steps are the hardest, and in the beginning, exercise will be more work than fun. But as you get into shape, you'll begin to tolerate exercise, then enjoy it, and finally depend on it.

Regular aerobic exercise will bring remarkable changes to your body, your metabolism, your heart, and your spirits. It has a unique capacity to exhilarate and relax, to provide stimulation and calm, to counter depression and dissipate stress.

So how does this actually work? The piece goes on:

The mental benefits of aerobic exercise have a neurochemical basis. Exercise reduces levels of the body's stress hormones, such as adrenaline and cortisol. It also stimulates the production of endorphins, chemicals in the brain that are the body's natural painkillers and mood elevators. Endorphins are responsible for the "runner's high" and for the feelings of relaxation and optimism that accompany many hard workouts — or, at least, the hot shower after your exercise is over.[17]

To put it another way: The next time you find yourself stressing about the news headlines, the investment markets, global macroeconomic trends ... try redirecting that energy toward movement. You may soon be in the best shape of your life — and worrying less.

Real Effort → Real Results

Now we have to be honest and state that exercise always takes effort. But that's a good thing. The simple act of activity is beneficial, even if you jog slower than normal. Your body and mind are still benefiting.

All of us would have to admit that in many facets of life we've coasted through a situation or potential challenge and gotten to the other side without exerting much real effort — only to find that cheaply obtained results weren't results at all.

If we had invested real work, we would have been happier with the outcome.

Active lifestyles naturally move us toward real results by design, because every step, every lift, every exerted breath is a challenge. It never comes cheap. That is why Phillips Brooks, the renowned Boston clergyman in the late 1800s, said, "Do not pray for easy lives; pray to be stronger men" (a line famously quoted by fellow Bostonian John F. Kennedy at the Presidential Prayer Breakfast of 1963).

Granted, it's not easy. Isaac Newton's First Law of Motion is still true, "Objects at rest tend to stay at rest." The only change comes when we force our "object" (our body) to get up from its static state and start moving.

If you allow your body to settle into inertia, it takes effort to interrupt that state. But once you do, the rewards will be priceless. As the physical therapists always say, "Movement is the best medicine."

The Silhouette in the Window

Every time I (Alex) am out on a run and pass a hospital or assisted-living facility, a renewed sense of mortality strikes me. I know dozens of people are up in those windows, watching me run by. They are most likely sickly, struggling with some health challenge, or perhaps even nearing life's end. They would like to be out doing what I'm doing, but cannot.

In those moments as I keep jogging down the street, I'm overwhelmingly grateful for my ability to get outside, inhale the fresh air, and run. Doing this while being observed by those who may wish with every ounce of yearning to do the same is poignant for me.

If we have the ability to be active and move, thereby improving our lives through exercise/movement, don't we have an inherent responsibility to do just that? In our opinion, the answer is yes. As Marvel comic book creator Stan Lee famously wrote in his Spider-Man comics, "With great power comes great responsibility." This applies in so many areas of life, and physical activity is one of them.

Get up and start moving—not only for yourself but also for all those who can't. Enjoy the bliss they can only dream of. Sure, it takes effort. But one day *you* may be the silhouette in the window, watching another person enjoying an active life and wishing you could join in—but alas, that window of opportunity has passed. Remember, if you find yourself in that assisted-living facility, a brisk run doesn't need to be your objective. But perhaps you can walk the property multiple times a day. Pushing yourself comes in all shapes and sizes. But the benefits are universal.

Don't Grow "Old"; Instead, "Age Young"

So often people in their fifties and beyond love to extol their position as "getting old" or "feeling their age." This tends to begin happening well before they actually would be deemed old by society, or at least appear to be "old" on the surface. These people tend to be more wrinkled, tired, stationary, and less energetic. They're missing out on the direct correlation between active lifestyle, positive thinking, and overall health.

How about deciding instead to "age young"? It's always shocking to meet folks in their seventies and even eighties who have signed up for some 5K race or who are heading out for a hike. Then there's the opposite—the grandma-and-grandpa types who look the part but don't even qualify yet for the senior discount! The contrast is striking.

What is the difference between these two types of people? An active lifestyle. Excuses abound among the sedentary: "I have a bulging disc ... my knees are bad ... my hips are bad...." But the truth is, no matter what your health situation, a more active lifestyle (unless clearly restricted by your doctor) will make you younger and healthier.

To quote the Harvard Medical School article again, "Exercise cuts the risk of heart attack, stroke, diabetes, colon and breast cancers, osteoporosis and fractures, obesity, depression, and even dementia (memory loss). Exercise slows the aging process, increases energy, and prolongs life."

So get up and live the life you want. It's right there; you just have to move to get it.

Have friends in every generation!

Key No.4 — Journaling

The minute you saw this chapter title, what stereotype went through your mind? An older, aristocratic lady with plenty of time on her hands writing down her various emotions? A grade-school child with a pencil scribbling in a red-covered diary with a lock, then hiding it under the bed?

If so, you've not explored the half of it. Hal Elrod, popular California podcaster and best-selling author, says in his book *The Miracle Morning*, "Writing in a journal each day, with a structured, strategic process, allows you to direct your focus to what you did accomplish, what you're grateful for, and what you're committed to doing better tomorrow. Thus, you more deeply enjoy your journey each day, feel good about any forward progress you made, and use a heightened level of clarity to accelerate your results."

We consider *journaling* to be a sister to *movement*, the topic of the previous chapter. Whereas exercise helps you physically, journaling is a workout for your mind and emotions. That's why we've included it as one of our ten keys to a fulfilling life after work. At the start, writing in a journal may seem more rudimentary, like exercise. However, if you keep going, you will find you not only enjoy it, but you need it.

Later in this chapter, we will make some suggestions on how to effectively journal. But with that said, we think the process is more important than the product. Just as we didn't lay out a seven-point exercise plan in the last chapter, we won't go so far as to say you need to write this or that in order to benefit. We will offer some suggestions to try and help you kick off a meaningful life of journaling, but it's up to you to discover for yourself.

We will tell you right now that your first journal won't resemble your fifth one. This is because, as you walk through life's ups and downs over time, you will tend to home in on the content you find most helpful.

No one is here to judge you. Some entries will be better than others. There will be lots of times you don't feel like doing it (just like any useful discipline). That's okay; do it anyway! Your journal is one of the few places you can go to *just be you.*

How Does It Help?

Writing is the least expensive counseling. Writing down your thoughts forces you to process and reflect, helping you to think more clearly around issues. Let's face it, life is a ball of emotions. It's hard and beautiful and messy and tiring and terrible and awesome. Writing helps you decompress and think more clearly about the challenges and issues you face, similar to the way that talking through a problem with a trusted friend or family member can help you better prepare for addressing it.

You know how there are times when something bad happens that elevates your blood pressure, and you really shouldn't respond right away? Taking the additional step of

Write down things you are thankful for.

writing these things down can really bring the breakthrough you're looking for on how to respond or handle a situation. Getting the problem out of your head and onto paper lightens the load, helps you think through the situation constructively, and affords you some freedom to get on with your life instead of continuing to stew on it for days. The award-winning poet and filmmaker Julia Cameron coined writing as "life's windshield wipers." Think of the wipers as clearing out the clutter in your mind. Having a place to write about the things that occupy your thoughts clears the way for you to be more effective.

> " Writing down your thoughts forces you to process and reflect, helping you to think more clearly around issues.

We human beings talk to ourselves at approximately 1,300 words per minute. We communicate verbally at roughly 150-200 words per minute. You may assume that we think at the same rate as we speak, but we don't. Our brains are much faster than our mouths. And unfortunately, most of our self-talk is negative.

It can be beneficial to just dump what's racing around the inside of your mind by writing about it. This leads to a cleaner windshield, so you can more effectively reach your goals for the day and stay out of a long debate with all your nagging thoughts. Do you prefer driving with a clean windshield or a dirty one?

The act of unloading or decompressing all of our complex emotions in real time helps avoid emotional buildup that can cause issues in the future. Yes, of course, you can find a human confidant to hear your deepest feelings or fears. If you want to pay, you can utilize a psychologist or counselor; these people serve an important role in many lives, as they allow their clients to unload mental burdens and quit internalizing whatever they are bottling up inside. Well, in a way journaling is like having your own personal therapist. Here you can uncork your raw, extremely personal emotions and decompress that built-up pressure within yourself.

Writing helps you self-reflect. Hectic lives leave little room for true reflection and consideration of your actions, fears, desires, disappointments, or challenges. These thoughts naturally appear and then disappear in our minds and thus are generally disregarded. But if you take the time to write them down, you've made more of a mental investment in them, which makes their presence last longer and carry more impact on your future actions.

For instance, imagine preparing to give a wedding toast or a speech. Do you simply think about what you plan to say, or do you write down your thoughts or specific items to address, and then review and fine-tune them? Which produces the better outcome?

Most of us prepare this second way, because our overloaded brains so easily lose track of valuable thoughts. But when we spend the time writing them down and reading them again, there is a permanence to the process; our brain tends to remember and use them in a different way. J. M. Barrie, the Scottish novelist and playwright (best remembered for creating the character Peter Pan), said it well, "The life of every man is a diary in which he means to write one story, and writes another; and his humblest hour is when he compares the volume as it is with what he vowed to make it." Only when we write down our reflections can we make these comparisons.

Writing can shift your perspective. Sheryl Sandberg (COO of Facebook, Inc.) lost her husband suddenly in 2015 from an unexpected heart failure. She's now a single mother while continuing to help run one of the largest companies on the planet. During this valley of her personal life, she turned to writing. At the end of each day she began writing down three things that gave her joy for which she was grateful. And it changed her life. Here's what she said about it during a commencement speech:

It is the greatest irony of my life that losing my husband helped me find deeper gratitude — gratitude for the kindness of my friends, the love of my family, the laughter of my children. My hope for you is that you can find that gratitude — not just on the good days, like today, but on the hard ones, when you will really need it.[18]

In this, her words are a great example of how journaling lets you take stock of those easily overlooked but brilliant pieces of life that are precious.

Writing tracks your progress. Reading your past writings is of tremendous benefit. It allows you to validate your progress and accomplishments. Retirement is a dangerous timespan where you'll question your effectiveness and purpose. Having the ability to reflect over the past year can really encourage you and validate the fact that you *are* doing good things and making good progress, even when it doesn't feel like it.

Reading your entries brings your objective voice into play and helps you recognize what was truly problematic, or what was just "noise" in your life that could have been neutralized. It's amazing how the simple act of journaling can become a truly self-soothing practice to refresh your outlook and mental state of being, helping you organize and take stock in your thoughts and life from a bird's-eye view, as opposed to solely living a reactionary life between your ears.

Both of us value this process even though we're not yet retired. For the retiree, it's even more critical, because you are no longer surrounded by the structure that more naturally led to progress.

Writing fosters creativity. Whether you're unpacking new ideas or simply writing what's on your mind, writing is a creative act that reduces stress. You are crafting your story. You are documenting your journey along the way.

When the word *creative* comes up, people tend to think of artists, graphic designers, writers, and painters. But as Stefan

Mumaw, author of six books on creativity, puts it, "Creativity is a skill, and any skill that you can undertake, the byproduct to it being a skill, is that you can get better at it."[19] An artist can be creative, but so can a mom, a mathematician, a salesperson, a CEO, or a retiree. Creativity is so important because it helps you become a better problem solver and allows you to grow in confidence. As you write through problems, you come at them differently than just chewing on them within your mind. Writing things down also helps you see that you can overcome failure. Once you see problems as survivable, you are more willing to enter unknown situations. Socrates was right when he said more than 2,000 years ago, "The unexamined life is not worth living."

> An artist can be creative, but so can a mom, a mathematician, a salesperson, a CEO, or a retiree.

Journaling creates a "written photo." We all use pictures to remember the past. Whether it's a place we visited, or our family gatherings through the years, photos bring a smile to our face and help us recall personal joys. Journaling is a complement to the old photo album, in that it tells the story the picture can't.

These precious nuggets can be used in many ways. They can bring joy as you reflect on past conversations with a child, parent, or spouse. They can be used by others to find strength and encouragement in an area of their life. They can add valuable detail to your story that would otherwise be forgotten.

A few years back I (Joel) took a day off work to go on a field trip with my oldest daughter. We headed 120 miles southeast to Bent's Old Fort National Historical Site. Constructed in 1833 along the Santa Fe Trail, it played a major role in opening the West. Trade brought together white adventurers, merchants of the Plains Tribes, and Mexicans. Relationships developed, and their lives were forever changed.

There are no photographs, of course, of Bent's Fort in its heyday. When you're visiting a place like this you want to believe it's true to its original state. You find yourself imagining the people in the rooms. What was life like without such basic necessities as a light switch? How did they build all their own equipment with fire and steel? Was Amazon delivery, like, *four* days back then?!

The original fort had long since crumbled, of course. Interestingly, building the replica had taken fifty-six years of alternating disappointment and triumph, and the persistent hopes and untiring work of many people. The rebuilders relied on descriptions. Fortunately, there was a sketch of the fort in the journal of Lt. James Aberts, an Army topographical engineer. He had arrived at Bent's Fort in 1846 and spent several months there while recovering from an illness. Aberts's careful drawing included many details including the layout of rooms and the fort's dimensions.

My daughter and I toured each of the rooms, and they were all intriguing. But the most special for me was one room where his journal was on display. It wasn't easy deciphering his cursive handwriting, but the information was priceless. Imagine if he didn't write it down? Imagine if Lewis and Clark didn't have a journal either.

Of course it's easy to look at this example and say, "Yeah, yeah, but we're not conquering the West. I'm just trying to get through dropping the kids off at school and handling all the day's emails!" You're correct—and I bet the pioneers didn't see heading out to hunt each day as interesting. After all, it was as rudimentary as driving to work. Whether you're just trying to make an impact on your kids, help friends and family around you, perhaps start a business, or keep a record of your life's challenges, your detail is unique and valuable—and it will likely grow in value as time marches on. We're never going to sit down with our kids, grandkids, or adult children and truly talk them through our adversity and life lessons as much as we would like. In fact, we may not even be around to meet some of our grandkids or certainly our great-grandkids. Maybe it's time to take a few less pictures and start writing down more lessons?

As we were writing this chapter, we mused about how pictures adorn our walls at home and how cool it would be if those people framed meaningful journal entries on how they became better by overcoming one of life's many mountains. Journals may be black ink on white paper, but they add more color than any photo could.

> **"** We may not even be around to meet some of our grandkids or certainly our great-grandkids. Maybe it's time to take a few less pictures and start writing down more lessons?

What Should an Entry Look like?

There's no exact blueprint for making a journal entry. If you engage in this practice, you'll eventually arrive at the most useful approach that works for you. But if you need a few suggestions for starters, here are some I've found useful over time as I've written some 2,000 pages or so:

Keep to just one page. When many people begin journaling, they love it. In fact, they love it too much, so they write like six pages. Not good. It's sort of like going to the gym on January 1. You haven't worked out in four years, but now you're a new you! So you work out for two hours ... and then you're too sore to go back. In journaling, keep it to one page at a sitting, and journal only a few days a week. Many people will tout daily journaling, but we don't think that's realistic with all we have going on. Like anything, it's good to have a day off, or sometimes your entries can get boring. Adding a day in between allows life to throw a few more curveballs your way.

Don't worry about perfection. No one's grading you here (unlike in most other areas of your life). No English composition teacher is here to judge you. You're free to not form every sentence correctly. You don't even have to worry about spelling! If someone reads it years after you're gone, they'll understand that a journal is informal and personal; this wasn't made to be published (unless you become famous). Meanwhile, it feels good to put something down that doesn't have to be perfect. This is just you and any lesson, feeling, or observation you would like to get onto the page. Big sigh.

Three ingredients. From looking back and re-reading my past journals, I have a pretty good idea of what I should be writing that I will find most useful in the future. Here are elements of my recipe:

- *Something light* — a brief bit about a positive thing you've done. It could be a trip or a memorable moment with a loved one or colleague. It might be as simple as noting you had a great weekend and why. Try to incorporate some informative details as you unpack your activities. For example, on a recent family vacation at the beach, we built a sandcastle. I could have simply said, "We went to the beach and built a sandcastle together." But what I actually wrote took on a larger meaning:

    "It was 72 degrees today, just warm enough to make a dip in the cold water refreshing and the breeze unnoticeable. James [my second oldest] jumped right in and started constructing the same sandcastle I had built the day before, with little help from him. It brought a smile to my face to watch him jump right in and try without Dad's help. John [my oldest son], who is all about soccer and thinks he dislikes art, jumped right in alongside James and had the cool and creative idea to add seashells to the castle. It was great to see him doing something imaginative as opposed to juggling a ball!"

    Hopefully you can see how I told a light story but incorporated in some useful details and traits to paint a better picture of who my kids are.

- *Something meaty* — Take a paragraph and go deeper on something you've learned or you're reflecting on. For me, I like to weave in my spiritual walk and document how I'm growing, what I'm learning, and what I'm struggling with. Sometimes I write about things that life happens to be teaching me as I age. These lessons can be very valuable for you as you reread. And if your family picks them up one day, they will be a treasured conversation with you.

- *Something for someone else* — I like to specifically pick certain events or discussions with my children, spouse, parents, or other loved ones that they may find valuable one day and that give me reason to smile when I reread it.

    I know I would love to be able to go back and read some of the conversations I had with my grandma and grandpa, or with my parents when I was younger. Unfortunately, nothing was ever written down, and so we look at the pictures and wonder what life was like behind the photo. What were we struggling with, what were we thinking about, what was good or bad?

    Journaling helps more than just you. It's an incredible gift you can use to encourage others. Not that you need to hand your granddaughter your journal, but if she happens to be dealing with a life challenge, you may be able to draw upon past entries to help her in a one-on-one conversation. For example:

    My daughter Claire was once struggling with friends in school. She was feeling disconnected and ganged up on a bit. I wrote down what she was dealing with and how she responded. She had told me that people can be mean but she's not going to be like that; she's going to treat people like she wants to be treated. She had said she would take this as a lesson on how not to act and would always try to make others feel included and welcome.

Well, I now see how far she's come. She's a leader at her school, serving other students through several outlets and making an impact. It's so useful to be able to recall all the details and themes that would have been simply forgotten or wouldn't fit in a nice picture frame. Now she can use what's written to help her see that overcoming challenges is a part of life. She's done it before, and she'll do it again.

Starting and Finishing

Now let's focus briefly on two important sections of the journal itself: the first entry and the summary at the end.

When you begin a new journal, open with a theme that sets the stage, encapsulating where you are and where you want to head in the next 200 pages. I always like to start with something I've learned over the last few years. My thought here is that if my wife or my kids ever open this up, I want them to be inspired.

So, who are you as a person? Who are you bringing into this collection of entries? Do you find yourself in a valley, at the summit, or somewhere on the ascent? What have you learned over the last journal, and to what do you aspire in the next journal? What are some goals? Pretend you're a wise old sage, and write something reflective or forward-thinking.

Then what about the end? Have you ever noticed that a whole year can go by and you don't feel like you've accomplished much? Sure, you may be able to remember the year's big event. But were there fractional improvements along the way? A summary on the final pages can make this much clearer.

Journaling is the counterweight to momentary feelings of *Another year went by and nothing really to show for it ... What difference am I making? ... Other people are accomplishing things, but I'm not.*

I will admit, this activity can take a bit of time (about four weeks in my case). I have to reread my journal. As I do so, I jot down on a note pad things that jump out at me. I categorize them by "Family," "Work," "Travel," "Personal Growth," "Challenges I've Overcome," and so forth.

I can tell you that there hasn't been a single year when I wasn't shocked by how much more was accomplished than what I had assumed or "felt." Thankfully, feelings don't beat hard cold facts. When you condense these items to four or five pages, it's powerful. They are like "encouragement concentrate." Not only is it a good reminder that you're doing more good than you think—a great counterbalance to your negative bias—but whenever you find yourself in a rut (and you will), you can simply pull out any year, read your summary, and you'll be encouraged.

This is one of the primary benefits of journaling: It has the strength to help vault you out of the hole you find yourself in.

But once you're above ground, don't stop. Keep writing.

Key No. 5 — Faith

Do you know who John Tyler was? No? Well then, surely you recognize Benjamin Harrison.

Actually, both of these gentlemen were presidents of the United States (Tyler was the tenth, Harrison the twenty-third). Maybe this goes to show that after just a couple of generations, 99 percent of us won't be remembered either. I mean, if presidents get forgotten, the prognosis isn't great.

Which raises an interesting question for us all: When the lights go out, is this life really all we have? If so, that's not good news for us. We may not even be remembered by our own family line.

If we camp on this thought for any length of time, it feels pretty discouraging. All the effort we put into making our mark, day in and day out, running and striving for meaning, seeking to leave a legacy, even serving others unselfishly ... and most of it won't be remembered?

So if our names and deeds are most likely going to fade to gray at the end of retirement, what are we striving for? What drives our value system (especially now that we've moved out from behind the façade of a corporate structure)? Why do we care about being good, or choosing right over wrong? Why does it still feel good to help someone?

We can tell you one thing: Human nature has not simply evolved toward inherent goodness. You don't have to be around many people very long to learn that we humans can be pretty messed up. Left to our own devices, we tend to wreak havoc on our own lives and those around us. This is one of the primary reasons for bulging Alcoholics Anonymous groups, high levels of depression, an American divorce every thirteen *seconds,* mass shootings, a drug epidemic, and quieter issues such as feeling unfulfilled or unhappy. The list goes on — and we've done it to ourselves.

As the ancient King David wrote, "Our days on earth are like grass; like wildflowers, we bloom and die. The wind blows, and we are gone — as though we had never been here."[20] If the lights go out, and we don't remember, and *they* don't remember — what was the point?

An Inner Quest

This would be a good time to ask ourselves the question "What is it inside of us that even wants to be remembered? Why does it disappoint us that we may not leave an impactful legacy where people talk about us for years to come?" The first answer is pride, and the second is our need to feel significant.

Psychology and faith share one fundamental agreement: Internal division leads to chaos and destruction. Of course, knowing that this internal strife exists, and knowing how to find alignment, are two very different things. Elizabeth Gilbert, popular journalist and author of *Eat, Pray, Love,* theorizes that "somewhere within us all, there does exist a supreme self who is eternally at peace." But read on, and you may find her observation rather ironic. She got very honest in a 2015 article for *The New York Times* entitled "Confessions of a Seduction Addict."

I careened from one intimate entanglement to the next — dozens of them — without so much as a day off between romances. Seduction was never a casual sport for me; it was more like a heist, adrenalizing and urgent. I would plan the heist for months, scouting out the target, looking for unguarded entries. Then I would break into his deepest vault, steal all his emotional currency and spend it on myself.

I might indeed win the man eventually. But over time (and it wouldn't take long), his unquenchable infatuation for me would fade, as his attention returned to everyday matters. This always left me feeling abandoned and invisible; love that could be quenched was not nearly enough love for me.[21]

Does it sound like she found that eternally peaceful supreme self? We are not making light of her division; we all have our own pitfalls. But it draws out the fact that this world is not going to help any of us solve the inner division. It will only compound the problem, as it did for Elizabeth Gilbert. With each striving came a greater thirst.

Let us make a bold statement here: We believe this humanly unbridgeable gap we're calling "division" is hardwired by God. It is a need for something greater that we cannot quench alone. It's as fundamental as the hardwiring of right and wrong, of gravity, or the sun continuing to rise. We are at best an "unfinished" project, consisting of a void unfillable by stuff, activities and efforts.

There are many acceptable vices we use to try and assimilate happiness and peace with our internal discontentment. They can be anything from shopping too much, distracting ourselves with certain hobbies, pouring ourselves into our work, an unhealthy focus on our children or grandchildren, an exaggerated emphasis on fitness, or overeating. These don't jump off the page as unhealthy, but the fact that they don't can in some ways be worse. It's easier to justify something to yourself when it's socially acceptable, making you less likely aware there's an issue in the first place.

Then there are darker items such as too much alcohol, substance abuse, physical and emotional affairs, lust, perhaps a false desire at the retirement age to "try something new with someone else." In a *USA Today* article, Teresa Collett, professor of law at the University of St. Thomas, wrote about the growing "gray divorce revolution."

> We live in a time where divorce is both common and socially acceptable. And while **general divorce rates are declining,** for those age 50 and above divorce rates have doubled since 1990. **For those age 65 and above the rates have tripled** (emphasis added).

Collett offers the primary cause:

> Gray divorce is more than a personal loss — it hurts families, friends, and communities. It is time for us to say so in our words and our actions. No one should stay in an unsafe relationship, but abuse is the cause of only a comparatively small proportion of divorces. **Far more common are divorces due to discontent — with our self, our spouse, or life in general.**[22]

Internal division is a problem we instinctively want to fix; all of us feel this way. But retirement brings a unique and potent combination: a shorter timeline coupled with more free time. It gives that inner voice of division a louder voice ... *FEED ME BECAUSE TIME'S ALMOST UP!* We are constantly trying to plug the hole or fill the gap or build a bridge to peace, to fulfillment.

It does not matter how much water you pour into a bucket if there's a hole in the bottom. We've seen some of the most well-intentioned, seemingly balanced people succumb to this illusion. The sad part is that we know from experience how the story ends if these mirages are indulged: badly, and with plenty of regret or perhaps worse. It is a misconception that young adults are the most prone to suicide. Among males, the suicide rate is highest for those aged sixty-five and older.[23] There's a darkness that comes when you realize you made a mistake and you're running out of time to fix it.

> ❝❝ It does not matter how much
> water you pour into a bucket
> if there's a hole in the bottom.

We have personally been close to many retiree divorces, which obviously come after almost a lifetime of marriage. The reasons vary, but they are all manifestations of internal division trying to be fulfilled in the unfulfillable.

Just Where Do I Fit?

One benefit of a personal faith is that it puts each of us in the proper place or order. We sense that we are wonderfully created. It's truly remarkable when we stop to think about all the parts and pieces that need to work together every day to keep our bodies alive. Faith removes the prideful stance of "it's all about me" and puts us in the proper posture for living a more meaningful and impactful life.

Some see a life of faith as laying down one's will for something else, and in some ways that is true. But if surrendering our pride and recognizing our place in the world order (as not the most important) can actually lead us toward a greater story, is that so bad? Not really.

Each of us would no doubt say, "I want the best for myself, for my spouse, for my kids, for my extended family, and for my clients." Very well; we're not saying you shouldn't have fun and shouldn't experience life's deep treasures as you try to pursue better versions of yourself. But the truth is that if we make ourselves into a god and go on chasing only our own desires, life doesn't turn out very good. The result is emptiness. On the other hand, living a life of faith, accepting that we can't explain everything, that something bigger than us created all this, creates the better result in life and for those we impact each day.

Granted, this requires a degree of trust. We have to be vulnerable enough to let our guard down and take this premise "on faith," so to speak. But faith is remarkable for those who earnestly pursue it. A definition in the Bible says, "Now faith is the substance of things hoped for, the evidence of things not seen."[24] You may find it odd to hear the two words *faith* and *substance* in the same sentence. After all, substance is tangible. Faith in God, believing in the afterlife, and attempting to follow the path God has laid before us all are, of course, intangible. But the effect of all these on our lives is quite real and recognizable. The *substance* is in the growth and outcome in a person's life that follows living one's faith.

In this book, we don't say this lightly or superficially, as if trying to convert someone to our personal beliefs. It is rather an earnest description of what we have seen firsthand in our own lives as parents, husbands, brothers, and of course financial planners.

One interesting connection between faith and retirement is acknowledging the brevity of life with the understanding that we are meaningful but so small in comparison to God. Having faith in God, we recognize that we indeed are not masters of the universe — by design we can't be! We have to set our pride aside, ask for forgiveness, thank God for certain things, perhaps even kneel or bow our heads or clasp our hands (in gestures of servitude and yielding) to pray. In that process, not only do we set aside silly underpinnings that permeate our society, but we also take a step toward identifying what fulfills us.

The Urgent, the Infinite

Erwin McManus, an accomplished author and pastor, tells a story in his book *The Last Arrow* that helps explain how the life beyond this one impacts us today. He was speaking at a 2009 conference in Mysore, India, alongside Devdutt Pattanaik, an Indian physician who calls himself a "mythologist."

> I was struck by his humorous and insightful contrast between Eastern and Western thought. His focus was on how the different myths that shape our worldviews affect us when we attempt to engage in business. But the implications go far beyond that.
>
> He contrasted the Indian mind-set, which approaches life more naturally with fuzzy logic, fluidity, and contextualization, with the Western mindset, which is more prone toward facts, logic, and standardization. Pattanaik pointed out that Hindus believing in reincarnation are not in a hurry, as they believe they have many lives to get things done, which is in contrast to the ancient Greeks, who believed that each person had only one life, and because of this, had a greater sense of urgency.
>
> Pattanaik wasn't advocating the rightness of either view; he was simply stating a fact that how we view our existence has a radical effect on our engagement in this life.

Erwin pondered what he was hearing and then proceeded to provide some of his own insight.

> Although there is much I admire about Eastern thought, I prefer the effect of what Pattanaik would call Western mythology. I am absolutely convinced that what we do in this life matters and that our time is our most precious commodity. There are no trial runs. In that sense, life does not allow us do-overs....
>
> Seeing the contrast between these two worldviews helps me understand the power of the Hebraic mind-set.

At the intersection of Western and Eastern worldviews the Hebrews were compelled by both the one and the infinite. We each have one life but this life has eternal significance. What we do in this one life has infinite implications, and beyond that, our stories are bigger than history. Our stories don't end when we do. They are only the beginning of much greater stories, the content of which we are completely unaware.

So in that sense we get the best of both worlds. Our deepest meaning must go beyond that which is confined to time and space, yet does not in any way diminish the importance of this moment. If the urgency of one life is what compels us to live our most heroic lives, then let's make the most of this one life each of us has. At the same time, we can only live that most heroic life well when we have a deep sense of the connectedness to that which is infinite and eternal.[25]

A New Kind of Habit

Being connected to something beyond ourselves is good. It can break the dastardly chains that confine our sense of purpose and meaning to only one life with no memory or purpose beyond. You are not here just passing time until someone turns the light switch off, striving to make sure you're remembered. You have a purpose beyond yourself but also a significant purpose within yourself.

Faith is a habit with an incredible power to shape our lives. Does it sound strange to describe faith as a habit? C. S. Lewis, the Irish-born scholar who tried to prove his atheism and eventually convinced himself that God exists, said that we "must train the habit of faith."[26] One commentator went on to say:

His point is a good one. All of us are caught every day inside the shifting moods of our emotions. If our schedule is thwarted by a slight rearrangement, our health fails us, our food digests badly, or the weather strikes as humid or foggy or simmering, we might begin to doubt everything. "This rebellion of your moods against your real self is going to come anyway. We have to be continually reminded of what we believe," says Lewis. "Neither this belief nor any other will automatically remain alive in the mind. It must be fed."[27]

So, what's your belief system? At this stage of life, are you still feeding it? Like any other habit, discipline, or state of mind discussed in this book, it doesn't grow on its own. And if it doesn't grow, it's not going to make the impact you need it to make.

What's really the point in making our last few decades great if it all simply ends when we do? Time goes by so fast. By yourself, you can't do enough to make it all you want it to be. We want to make sure that we have a wonderful retirement and that we then catapult into something far greater. Without faith, life can be void of an ultimate life-purpose; it becomes an elusive, time-wasting struggle to find lasting fulfillment in the wrong places. Knowing that time is fleeting and the sand in our hourglass has almost trickled to the bottom, we are caught in an internal struggle to handle the reality of *It's almost over* and *I haven't found it yet.* So, we move on to the next thing hoping for a better result.

But how sweet it is when we know the last drop of sand in that hourglass is but a release into something beyond our wildest dreams.

Ups and Downs

Now of course, living a life of faith isn't always easy. You don't arrive at faith and launch every day with a wonderful feeling inside. It doesn't help you explain why a loved one may suffer or your kids and grandkids may struggle. It doesn't fit in a perfect little box where life is just lovely.

Don't be surprised if your faith journey isn't perfect. Bad things will still happen. Good things will also happen. We live in a terrible and beautiful world, the complexities of which simply cannot be explained until one day when we meet God face to face.

One writer who experienced both the good and the terrible in his own life had this to say about living a life of faith. But first a bit of background. Originally called Saul of Tarsus, he was a Jewish leader who was strong on religion—and void of faith. He knew what to say or what to eat or what not to do. He went so far as to persecute and even oversee the imprisonment and sometimes murder of those following a revolutionary leader named Jesus. God was so bold as to do a miracle in Saul's life by blinding him as he was walking one day, speaking to him, and then changing his name to Paul. (There's more to the story if you care to read it in the Book of Acts.)

Paul stopped worshiping his religious practices, flipped the script, and turned to a life of faith. In fact, he went on to confound his Jewish associates by preaching faith all over the Mediterranean world (a certain affront to their beliefs); he was also the second largest contributor to the New Testament, the portion of the Bible where grace and mercy reign. Talk about an about-face.

Paul's biography demonstrates that we can all change. We don't have to be a victim of our past, which for many of us has already stolen so much. It doesn't get to have a say in our future if we don't want it to. Faith gives us the courage to change and the confidence to know it's going to matter.

> ❝ We don't have to be a victim of our past, which for many of us has already stolen so much. Faith gives us the courage to change and the confidence to know it's going to matter.

Now hear Paul's inspiring piece regarding faith in action:

Let love be genuine. Abhor what is evil; hold fast to what is good. Love one another with brotherly affection. Outdo one another in showing honor. Do not be slothful in zeal, be fervent in spirit, serve the Lord. Rejoice in hope, be patient in tribulation, be constant in prayer. Contribute to the needs of the saints and seek to show hospitality.

Bless those who persecute you; bless and do not curse them. Rejoice with those who rejoice, weep with those who weep. Live in harmony with one another. Do not be haughty, but associate with the lowly. Never be wise in your own sight. Repay no one evil for evil, but give thought to do what is honorable in the sight of all. If possible, so far as it depends on you, live peaceably with all. Beloved, never avenge yourselves, but leave it to the wrath of God, for it is written, "Vengeance is mine, I will repay, says the Lord." … Do not be overcome by evil, but overcome evil with good.[28]

Can any of us think of a better set of values to anchor the post-career years? Probably not. We can hardly do what is written here without finding fulfillment.

Jumping ahead twenty centuries, we'll leave you with one of the all-time famous movie quotes by Andy Dufresne in the movie *The Shawshank Redemption:* "I guess it comes down to a simple choice, really. Get busy living or get busy dying."

Key No.6 — Learning

In an earlier chapter we talked about vacations needing a counterbalance to serve their intended purpose. We said that if your whole life's a vacation, then you don't have true vacations anymore. It's a self-defeating cycle—similar to our concept of the occasional lazy morning, which can occur only in the context of "not-lazy mornings."

If the current season of your life isn't properly planned, the most common result will be to run out in search of part-time or full-time employment again. That's the "easy button," so to speak. All you have to do is go get hired somewhere, and you'll get back to a schedule, a reason to get up, people to interact with, a paycheck (whether you need it or not), a sense of seasonality and texture to your life, vacation time again, a recognized role in a larger strategy or objective … you'll feel useful again.

There is a more fulfilling route, but it's harder. Learning is the best surrogate to reentering the labor force in search of something meaningful. The Latin word *surrogare* translates to mean "elect as a substitute." It's a piece of the counterbalancing puzzle you're trying to assemble. Mahatma

Gandhi set the stage nicely when he said, "Live as if you were to die tomorrow. Learn as if you were to live forever."

Another Cornerstone

Learning is another cornerstone habit. If pursued meaningfully, it has the power to improve other areas of your life without much additional effort. After all, that's what a cornerstone habit is: something that reinforces other areas of your life automatically, providing collateral benefits.

Imagine someone who has always wanted to help others who are struggling in their marriages. She derives great benefit herself from the time she spent with her own counselor many years prior, and always thought she would be good at it. But she just hasn't had the time during her working years to ramp up her capabilities through education in order to pursue a desire that pays next to nothing.

Once retired, she decides some formal classes would be fun and challenging while equipping her with the necessary tools. So she enrolls at the local college. She is pleased to meet a few other "more mature" students on the campus; after all, learning isn't just a young person's game anymore.

She thoroughly enjoys the courses, because as it turns out, learning is a lot more fun when you don't *have to* do it. After two years of study, she is formally licensed as a marriage and family counselor. She then accepts a volunteer role at a local nonprofit that provides these costly services for free to a struggling demographic. Yes, that's correct — she's *paid* for an education that she then turns around and gives away for free. (That's what you call a "purpose.")

Here are some of the collateral benefits that learning has brought to her life:

- She enjoyed the rigors of the schooling challenge; she liked being tested.
- But she also enjoyed the seasons off (Thanksgiving, Christmas, spring break, summertime). Her calendar had texture.

- She enjoyed the victory that came with accomplishing a goal.
- She forged new meaningful relationships with people she was able to study alongside and work alongside.
- She was surprised at how much she enjoyed speaking into the lives of younger students in the group portions of their classes.
- Now she loves putting her resume into practice and helping others.
- She receives tremendous fulfillment from the concept of "doing this for free" because she wants to give back.
- She now gets to enjoy vacations as much as she did during her career, because every day isn't a vacation!
- She has lots of good stories to journal about and revisit later in life as she reflects on her legacy.
- She is incredibly thankful she didn't forgo this opportunity in exchange for the easy answer of going back to a paying job.

We could keep going … but it all started with learning.

Formal Paths, Informal Paths

Maybe you don't have a personal wish like this woman's to draw upon. No problem—just pick something that has always interested you, and start doing it. Trust that the purpose will unfold even if you don't have a master plan. Learning is as much about the journey as the destination.

In our roles as financial advisors, we've found that people generally hesitate to try new things. They tend to stick to the way they've always lived. If they can't foresee the final result from the beginning, they don't want to step out and try.

Many people have a vague sense of something they would like to try but don't really know where to start or what the ultimate use of the tool will be. Both are perfectly fine. Learning is an adventure; it can take us places we weren't expecting to go. As Socrates said, "Education is the kindling of a flame, not the filling of a vessel."

When you step away from the structure that has been your life for years upon years, it's time for something new and exciting. It's time to learn new skills and knowledge that you can give to a world in need of innovation and good will. If you are still passionate about what you did in your career and feel it gave you skills that can still make an impact, by all means use them—but try drawing upon those old reserves in a new way. If you're a physician, why not take some time volunteering with Doctors Without Borders in a developing country? If you're an engineer, could you lend your expertise to a nonprofit working in a new place or serving an unfamiliar demographic? If you're a financial advisor, why not look for ways to educate the aspiring younger generation who knows little about finance and its importance for a proper start?

> "Education is the kindling of a flame, not the filling of a vessel." —Socrates

Learning and adventuring toward new horizons in retirement is such an exciting proposition. The two of us have observed many of our clients undertaking entirely new endeavors and loving the purpose and fulfillment they bring. But remember there may still be so much to learn even within the same vein that you are accustomed to. Don't think you need to undertake some obscure new thrill-seeking hobby if that's not what you are about.

Personal Benefits

A recurring theme throughout this book is the idea that great things can unfold when you remove yourself from what is comfortable. Just as a physically active lifestyle keeps your body fit, learning has been shown to keep your mind young and healthy. Researchers from the University of Texas at Dallas took 221 adults ages 60-90 and separated them into three distinctive groups. Each group was tasked to do fifteen hours of mental activity each week over the course of three months.

The first group had to undertake new activities they had never attempted before — say, quilting or digital photography.

The second group was tasked with doing familiar at-home things such as completing a puzzle or listening to classical music. The third group spent their fifteen hours each week out in social activities, such as group field trips and going together to entertainment.

The researchers found that only the first group — the ones challenged with new activities that required them to learn — showed clear cognitive improvement, especially in the area of memory.[29] It is not enough to simply be stimulated or engaged in an activity. Learning helps you stay mentally young and sharp.

Dig Deep

The learning process has changed drastically in the past century. Previously, someone who wanted to study something usually had to travel to a library to find books on the subject, or correspond directly with an expert. Today, any information about anything can be found instantly online. Not only that, but you can connect directly with groups of people who share a common interest, no matter how obscure. This is convenient — but there's very little investment in obtaining information that comes "free." Much less is learned if you don't have to work at it.

Apps are coming soon that will be able to translate languages in real time so you'll have your own pocket translator anywhere on the planet, forgoing the need to learn another language. The technology and application to the world is remarkable. But learning and all the benefits it offers are beginning to be bypassed.

You still have the ability to deeply explore any topic, if you are willing to make the effort. As Alexandre Dumas wrote in *The Count of Monte Cristo*, "I don't think man was meant to attain happiness so easily. Happiness is like those palaces in fairy tales whose gates are guarded by dragons: we must fight in order to conquer it."

So get fully immersed in whatever you want to understand; explore what triggered your curiosity in the first place. Don't settle for a Wikipedia explanation or the first hotlink that pops up. Dig beneath the surface-level information, pushing your brain to adapt to the unfamiliar. Benjamin Franklin said: "Tell me and I forget. Teach me and I remember. Involve me and I learn." Get involved; you'll be amazed at what you'll gain.

Ask yourself, "What am I genuinely curious about?" We are all so different, so don't try to conform to what society thinks is interesting or what your other retired peers are doing. What makes you say, "Wow, that's amazing!" or "It would be so interesting to _____"? People who explore some niche idea or unique undertaking purely out of curiosity and a desire to learn are genuinely fulfilled. It's always very evident when a person is passionate about something. Do you speak with excitement and fascination about your passions or something you are currently learning? There literally isn't enough time to explore all the mind-blowing avenues of learning that are waiting to engage and fascinate you.

Doing something new means you will not initially be good at it. But as you comprehend enough about the subject to see how inept you are, that void teaches you a lot about yourself. Do you have the gumption to press on and seek the answers or skill required to pursue that passion? Or will the path of least resistance tempt you to stop?

> " Doing something new means you will not initially be good at it. But as you comprehend enough about the subject to see how inept you are, that void teaches you a lot about yourself.

If you stay focused on mastering some new endeavor because you are passionate about it, you will feel immensely good when you reach a level of competency that you know, deep within yourself, was *earned*. Retirees need some wins under their belt more than anyone. You've lived too long to gain benefit from superficial praise or flattery from an outside source. The pat-on-the-back comes now from within. To feel accomplished, you first have to ... accomplish!

On the Road Again

One couple we know, after decades in the workforce, liquidated most of their possessions (except their investment portfolio, of course), purchased a nice camper, and decided to be nomads for a year or two. They had lived in the same city for most of their careers, employed at the same companies. But now their goal became to see all of the United States, learn its history, and experience its beauty.

They began by mapping their course to hit northern national and state parks during the summer and then head south in the winter, zig-zagging across the country while stopping in to see family along the way. They're the kind of people who pull over at each overlook and read the entire historical sign with real curiosity.

It's been almost five years now, and they continue this lifestyle, despite having plenty of money to stay home and be "normal retirees." Every time we speak with them on the phone (when they have cellular service, that is), it sounds something like this: "Well, we are at ____ National Park for a couple months. Bill tried fly fishing and is learning how to tie his own flies. I'm volunteering at the campground site handing out informational pamphlets about the area. I also have a new stack of books I'm eager to start."

Notice that they don't have "learning" per se as an objective. They are merely following their curiosity and hearts into unknown, new endeavors that they think they might like. Along the way (literally), they are venturing into countless new sources of learning and intrigue.

Others hit two birds with one stone by blending their own travel interests with their grandparenting. A California couple has said to each grandchild, "When you get to be twelve years old, we'll take just you—no siblings, no parents—on a special trip all the way across the country to Washington, D.C." (Notice: not Disney World or Six Flags.) "We'll explore all the amazing buildings there, the White House, the monuments, the Smithsonian, learning all about our great country."

But you don't even have to buy airplane tickets to enhance your knowledge. We heard about a CEO who, once his busy life in the executive suite wrapped up, decided he wanted to read a biography of *every* U.S. president. Not just the famous ones—Washington, Jefferson, Lincoln—but also those about whom he knew next to nothing. What major challenges had they faced? How did they make decisions? What were their greatest victories? Their most crushing defeats? Did they have a faith in God to sustain them, or not? What kind of family life did they have? The man found great enrichment through this pursuit.

But First—a Caution

Whatever the channel for learning—a college class, a book, a podcast, a TED Talk, a news report—we have to be careful to evaluate the source. Every professor, author, speaker, and even close friend has his or her own perspective. We must stay alert to biases and slants that influence the exchanges. Do we really want to absorb this material and embrace it as our own? Maybe it's worthy, but then again maybe it's flawed. Maybe this information is valid, but then again maybe it's a case of "spin."

Our society has become so accustomed to letting the news tell us how to feel that we almost don't know what to think apart from it. Too many times the only decision we've kept for ourselves is what side to take. A recent example of this in the financial world was the summer of 2019's "inverted yield curve." You would have thought that every person was suddenly an expert economist! We had clients who didn't even know what a yield curve was telling us, "Now that it's inverted, a recession is coming!" Guess where they learned that … yup. Some talking head on one of TV's business channels.

The funny (or actually sad) thing is, people who believed it missed out on one of the best investment return years in a long time. We've actually joked with some of our clients about doing exactly the opposite of what the "experts" were telling them, and they'd be wealthy. Beware of any information outlet that has some axe to grind (which is a large majority of them, whether on TV or Facebook or your neighbor).

The other challenge, in addition to this media narrative being accepted as "normal" or "factual," is that there's not much else readily available unless you work at it a bit. As we said earlier, you have to dig deeper. For example, I can easily turn my Sirius XM to Fox or CNN or NPR, but it's not very easy to dial up an awesome leadership podcast. I have to remember to download it at some point, or stream it in my car and hope my service is good. Isn't it curious that good, fulfilling things are harder to find? It's almost as though someone stacked the deck against us. It's like how fast food is everywhere, but finding a wholesome meal takes more effort.

We're not saying you need to bury your head in the sand and ignore world events or even stop reading the newspaper. What we're hoping to convey is that you should stay keenly aware of the junk that's intertwined with media bias. For every portion of junk, you need to add two portions of value to your intake. The news narrative can be likened to a tasty burger and fries. When you're hungry, it sounds so tempting. So go ahead and enjoy a burger once in a while; we do. But commit yourself to other intake items for which you'll need to search a bit: that good podcast series, that book you need to order because your friend suggested it, turning off the screen because you've had too much. These are all your fruits and vegetables.

Engaging daily with biased content while ignoring the other will have a similar effect on your mind that eating a burger and fries each day would have on your health. We must guard it and make balanced decisions. Don't let the news become who you are. The pontification you indulge will most certainly lead you away from what you're hoping to become.

The average retiree watches forty-nine hours of television a week. And most of the channels come from publicly traded corporations. These businesses have revenue targets to hit and stockholders to please. Unfortunately for you and me, good news simply doesn't sell as well as bad or shocking news. And if it doesn't sell, then the market price of advertising goes down, which hurts profitability for the company. The media bosses understand this very well; they know what will get you to watch, and that's what they air.

Don't let someone else's bottom line color the way you see the world or lead you to make poor decisions. After all, you can't control politics, or society, or what's going on in the Middle East, or the stock market, or what happens with international trade. You can only control what you choose to do with your time. At the end of life, you're guaranteed to never say, "I wish I would have spent more time watching bad news instead of investing in myself, my family, and my friends."

> **" Don't let someone else's bottom line color the way you see the world or lead you to make poor decisions.**

Always keep learning—from intelligent, trustworthy sources. This is a vital part of a successful and fulfilling post-career life. If you're not experiencing life, you're not learning. And if you're not learning, you're slowly dying from the disease called "retirement."

You've probably heard the statement "There's only one you." Well, actually, that's not true. There are at least two of you. Remember the old cartoon about the angel and the devil, each of them whispering on someone's opposite shoulder? Even children understand at a very young age that two different trains of thought are rumbling through their minds — otherwise, the cartoon wouldn't make sense. We understand this intuitively.

But one thing we *don't* understand intuitively is that the darker voice is much louder than the lighter, quieter voice. To illustrate the imbalance, take a moment and picture the devil as ten times larger than the angel. Deep inside our brains is an area called the limbic system, which houses our emotional responses and memory. Then there's the neocortex, which handles what scientists refer to as our "higher functions" such as critical thinking, reasoning, and learning.

The limbic system is the home of our fight-or-flight response, a survival mechanism for responding quickly to threats. The neocortex processes our higher learning functions much slower.

If we're confronting a saber-toothed tiger, we don't have time to consider all the possible strategies to escape; we just need an immediate fight-or-flight decision! But in situations requiring rational thinking, we need to listen to the neocortex voice a little longer. Take, for example, financial decision making. As advisors, we occasionally have clients reacting in fear and wanting to "get out of the market now!" Their brain has produced an emotional cocktail, and they are ready to run.

The limbic system has led to many poor decisions when the neocortex should have been leading. We're not saying the limbic system is all bad; the issue is rather in knowing how and when to interact with it. And that calls for a healthy measure of *awareness.*

You might call our emotional side our "inner teenager," while our neocortex represents our "adult self." Teenagers know everything, right? At least they think they do, and so does our limbic system ... if we let it.

Who's Talking?

Just knowing that our rational brain (the "lighter" voice) is at a disadvantage is already an advantage. Given a hearing, it can make more sense of many situations. We will even ask ourselves, *Why did I do that? Why did I react that way?* If you know that the voice of discernment (which is something you desperately need) is at a tremendous disadvantage to the voice of ignorance or quick reactions, you're already lightyears ahead of everyone else and better equipped to favor your lighter side.

When a family sits down for dinner each evening, certain personalities are always heard at the table, while others aren't. If we're aware of this, we try to make space for the quieter voices to be heard. Otherwise, they will be drowned out.

Awareness is when you decide to let the lighter voice be at least on par with the louder voice. Please note, this does not come naturally. Awareness has to be constantly chosen; it's generally not something that is learned or obtained. If you learn something, it comes naturally in the future. But awareness will never come naturally.

So the need is to keep self-reflecting, understanding what your emotional responses are, why you feel that way, and separating yourself from those emotions to be more measured and clear-thinking when you do respond. Keep in mind that this in no way means trying to *limit* emotions; after all, emotions are fundamental to our existence. It's rather pausing to understand them, which will create substantial results in your life.

> Keep self-reflecting, understanding what your emotional responses are, why you feel that way, and separating yourself from those emotions to be more measured and clear-thinking when you do respond.

One of Warren Buffett's many mentors, Tom Murphy (former CEO of Capital Cities/ABC, Inc.), told him early in his career, "Warren, you can always tell someone to go to hell tomorrow." In other words, you don't have to let those words fly today. Buffett said that was "one of the best pieces of advice I've ever received."

The takeaway message is that, whether in high-powered negotiations or around the kitchen table, it's good to be mindful of your emotional reactions and take some time before responding. If you pause and take stock of your emotions, you're more likely to choose the rational approach. You'll wind up with better results and fewer enemies.

In retirement, you are held accountable much less. You no longer operate within the same professional/social circle of colleagues with whom you spent the majority of your time. Even the most self-*unaware* person in a business generally had to at least try to be a reasonable person in the office or boardroom.

But once you retire, you move outside those etiquette guide rails; you're free to act however you like! You don't need to worry about being fired or creating a grudge with someone in your company that could negatively affect your future. You can now sound off (in person, on the phone, on Facebook) as vehemently as you want. In this new season, nobody holds you accountable but yourself. All the more reason to be aware of your behavior and strive to be as rational as possible in each situation.

Awareness in Action

Awareness has many levels. An obvious one we can all think of is the friend or family member who just won't stop talking, mostly about *their* life and *their* problems. We think to ourselves, *They're just so unaware!*

We've all known someone who is just rude in general; they're not necessarily mean at heart, but they say the strangest things at the wrong time. They're clueless about their faux pas.

You may think such cases aren't that big of a deal and can simply be tolerated. You may tell yourself, "So I steal the dinner conversation with friends most of the time — they don't mind...." Actually, they do mind, and it does matter. If you live your life this way, you'll find yourself being avoided by others, and this could be a very big deal. How we carry ourselves can affect our relationships, and if we don't have relationships that are truly helpful and not just a façade, we will suffer not only mentally but physically. If no one wants to be around you, that's a problem, and it's usually attributed to a lack of awareness. As Warren Buffet wrote in his 1987 letter to shareholders, "If you have been in a poker game for a while, and you still don't know who the patsy is, you're the patsy."

The good news is that this can be changed! I (Joel) was having coffee with my close friend Joe, who filled me in on a recent dinner he and his wife, Maddie, had endured with another couple they've known for years. Both couples are retired, so they go out to eat together frequently.

However, John and Kate have been embarrassing them at meals over the last few years. Regardless of where they are or what they order, they always manage to complain about the food and harass the server. Joe and Maddie are the type of people who understand that, even if the dinner's not perfect, the waitress likely has life problems just like everyone else. She's probably tired and in the middle of working really hard and dealing with other guests who are unaware.

Obviously the meal and service isn't bad everywhere this foursome goes. The complaining mode is simply who John and Kate have allowed themselves to become. There's a kinder, more positive John and Kate inside them that could absolutely decide to change. But left unattended, they are heading down a path to isolation and miserable mindsets.

Joe looked right at me as he sipped his latte and said, "We're going to give them one more try — but if it happens again, we're done."

John and Kate have a disease. They most likely take this unawareness with them into every area of life. As the apostle Paul wrote twenty centuries ago, "Don't you know that a little yeast leavens the whole batch of dough?"[30] A little unawareness can affect the whole outcome of your actions. These "not-so-big deals" are simply manifestations of other, more deeply rooted awareness issues.

Are you aware that you can improve? That all of us can learn good things from one another? Or do you believe you have "arrived?"

Awareness Is for All

We've talked earlier about all of us being leaders, regardless of our role. You don't need to be a CEO to be a leader. If you're a grandma, you're a leader; if you're a wife, you're a leader; if you're post-career, you're still a leader. The most important quality of a leader is their ability to be self-reflective or aware, to understand that they aren't God's gift to humanity and that they may have some changing to do.

Remember, life isn't about beating anyone; it's simply about a daily pursuit of a better version of you. Show me someone who never changes and has always been stuck in the same old ways, and I'll show you someone who's not only a poor leader but totally unaware. Again, awareness serves as our auditor here. If we aren't aware, we have no idea where to look to improve.

Another deeply ingrained manifestation for many of us is mindless spending. Overspending can be outright dangerous for the retiree. Most Americans are accustomed to spending the money they have (and don't have). There's rarely a pause button when it comes to shopping in our somewhat compulsive retail society. Consumerism is two-thirds of the U.S. economy, so we may all be guilty of this one!

The issue is not spending or shopping, it's being mindful when you do. Do you really need X, or is it a "want"? Is the immediate gratification of buying this new object worth more to you than the security and potential flexibility that the money would afford you later on? Is the new purchase destined to be jammed into a donation bag within a year or two? There's a good chance!

Awareness of spending can be a major hurdle for those leaving careers where it was never an issue to keep spending, because the money spigot was always "on." Now all of a sudden, income is a trickle, and your spending comes directly out of your finite stash of resources. This can be an anxious process for some as they worry about spending but continue their habit of spending unnecessarily.

An increased level of introspection into your own spending will help you discern what is actually worthwhile. If you are mindful about purchases, the ones you make will truly be special, while the ones you decide to forgo were the wasteful ones that were going to be frivolous. This process can directly reduce spending-induced anxiousness that many retirees seem to quietly combat. There's no measuring stick without awareness.

The Voice in Your Head

Self-talk has immense power over our emotional state and general wellbeing. The silent "voice in our head" speaks at a much faster rate than our mouth ever could, and it tends to control our moods. Our self-talk can either be positive or negative, but without mindfulness, much of the time it is negative.

The Mayo Clinic lists some of the health benefits of positive thinking as it relates to self-talk. They include increased life span, lower rates of depression, greater resistance to catching colds, and better coping skills during hardship and stress.[31] It's shocking what a little bit of optimistic thinking can do!

If you are full of self-doubt and self-criticism, try some self-acceptance for a change. You'll find much of your negative self-talk is complete fiction. As you become aware of your self-talk and listen intently to it, you'll quickly discover whether it's optimistic or pessimistic. Then take the time to consider why it is what it is, and challenge any pessimism that arises. This will not only make you genuinely happier (and healthier) but also a much more measured and rational investor.

The Mental Courtroom

Awareness can be likened to a mental courtroom — except there's a twist. This courtroom isn't orderly; the two sides don't get equal time to argue their cases. Here, the judge allows the plaintiff to make ten statements for every one from the defendant. Yes, it's unfair, but it's the law in this particular state, the "State of Mind."

The plaintiff is Mr. Emotional; the defendant is Mrs. Rational. Not only does Mr. Emotional get to talk more, he even gets to raise his voice far above Mrs. Rational and at a much higher speed without being held in contempt--unless of course you as the judge decides to do so. That's right, you're the judge. You're the one ruling on every decision in your life.

We should say that no one is exempt from this imbalance. You don't get to change the law of Mr. Plaintiff having 10-to-1 leverage. You merely get to increase your discernment to create the counterbalance. Let's say someone does something to you that is incredibly irritating. You are ready to bring down the hammer, and you have every right to do so. You wouldn't be incorrect; actually, you would be justified. However, it doesn't mean you should, right?

We have a simple rule as it relates to email or text messaging. If you find yourself in an elevated moment (and you'll know when you are), go ahead and type that passionate response—but then save it; don't send it. Marinate on it for twenty-four hours, then come back and read it again. If you still agree, send it.

The funny thing is, the message almost never gets sent. Why? Mrs. Rational had time to speak. If it's 10 to 1, Mrs. Rational needs some *time*. Eventually, you *discern* that even though you have every right to send it and your points are correct, it doesn't add any value to your life, and therefore it's time to just let it go and move on to things that will make a good impact in people's lives rather than wallow in life's pettiness. Sending that response could have tied you up for weeks, stewing on it, wondering what the reader's response would be, then responding to the response....

This is only a small example. Sometimes the issues are much larger than a written attack on you. Regardless, the rules of the court are the same. As the judge, you are tasked with creating fair decisions while putting up with an annoying, overheard plaintiff—all day long all the time. These are the rules under which we have to play the game. The first major step in being able to play this game well is understanding that the rules are not in your favor. This is called *Awareness,* and it's "table stakes" if you are to live a fulfilling and impactful final third of your time here on earth.

One interesting observation: As we age, we tend to compound in one direction or the other. What that means is that the biases we've built or the rational or irrational mindsets to which we've succumbed are more pronounced when we're older. We all probably know someone who would be considered a wise old sage, who discerns well, and has managed losses and wins equally well. Conversely, we all probably know someone who has no filter, tends to wreak havoc along the way, saying whatever they want or feel. As we age, our filters tend to get thinner and we more quickly manifest who we truly are, due to our lack of awareness.

We need to be uber-sensitive to this progression.

Financial Astuteness

Investing and financial planning is a unique, highly complex profession, and the outcomes have long-term, serious ramifications for any household or organization. It's hugely important to get right.

But unlike surgery, engineering, law, or rocket science, it's an undertaking that anyone can attempt, and have some luck initially. It's easy to open an investment account, read some articles, and start buying stocks or bonds. It's easy to read an article about Social Security, estate planning, or retirement accounts and start making decisions about what you plan to do.

The problem is that the result can end the same as if you attempted to be the lead surgeon in a liver transplant, or chief engineer for NASA's Mars missions, or the lead counsel in a lawsuit. Investing can seem to be easy, until it's not. And when it's not, life trajectories are irreversibly changed. Awareness of one's own strengths and where one needs guidance isn't as clear with investing and financial planning as it is in other facets of life. But it's just as poignant. If investment management is a true passion and feels purposeful to you, then by all means jump into the deep end. But chances are there are so many other things that make you feel fulfilled that you could spend your time doing.

To paint the picture: The average U.S. investor's return over the 20 years ending December 31, 2018, came to just 1.9% per year (versus 5.6% per year for the S&P 500 index).[32] Why? Because individual investors do a very poor job of managing their emotions. They see investing as an equation to follow, a surface-level undertaking: "I'll read some articles, just buy and hold an index, it's cheap and easy" — until a recession hits, or they hear about something better from a "smart neighbor" or close friend, or they begin to squirm when things get bumpy and retirement is nearing.

Your nest egg is the financial culmination of your blood, sweat, and tears throughout your career. It's the excess proceeds of effort that you have painstakingly set aside for your future. Honestly, how could one not be crazy-emotional and protective of this? When emotional tendencies (which we all grapple with, since they're a part of human nature) drive investment decisions, it's always a negative thing.

This simple truth about financial awareness is shrouded by so many influences in our society. There's the classic commercial by some large online trading platform presenting a super-wealthy investor in a beautiful house with a tremendous view, clad in a cozy cashmere sweater, sipping a steaming cup of coffee, and clicking a few buttons achieving trading success. Or it's the always confounding "financial expert" who wants to sell his or her trading strategy, stock pick newsletter, or how to get rich quick in the market scheme. The ironic part is if they truly had a treasured strategy or nugget, the last thing they would do is sell it to the world, right? I mean, why would a great stock picking strategy need to sell a newsletter for $15 a month? It's odd. Because it's not true. It doesn't work, and because it doesn't work they need to make revenue trying to sell their failed strategy to you. Otherwise they would just implement their own strategy for themselves and become wealthier than any pile of book sales or newsletter subscriptions. (You wouldn't believe how prevalent this is.)

Biases Shape Our Outlook

It's always a little counterintuitive to understand that perhaps the largest variables dictating our future financial outcomes are behavior and emotions, especially for retirees who can't just put their head down and keep working and saving when times get challenging. Numerous emotional biases about money and retirement have been well documented and researched. Here are a few commonplace biases to keep in check when measuring your own state of mind.

Anchoring: This cognitive bias occurs when initial information or data is "anchored" in the brain so firmly that the person does not adjust when new information comes along. Whenever you hear someone say, "Well, the market is high now" or "The market is due for a correction because it's at ____ level!" they are merely anchoring to some prior numerical level without understanding what conditions have produced the current market. During bull markets, anchoring happens the entire climb; every week the market hits "a new all-time high" and is declared "overvalued" strictly because of its new level, not because of any factual reasoning. The share price of any investment never indicates whether it is overvalued or undervalued. Only computing the ever-changing intrinsic value of the business in question does that.

Confirmation Bias: This is when someone has a preconceived notion or belief about something, and then looks for evidence to support that conclusion, even if a vast amount of data explicitly points elsewhere. When someone has that emotional "gut feeling" that the market is going to crash, and they watch a "breaking news" segment about impending doom that directly follows an interview of a world-renowned economist explaining the strength of the economy, the investor ignores the economist and doubles down on their belief that a catastrophe is right around the bend.

On the other hand, this bias can result in overconfidence, because we can continually get data and reports that appear to confirm the decisions we have made. With confirmation bias we hear what we want to, not necessarily the facts.

Being able to objectively challenge an investment thesis is imperative to bypass confirmation bias. Charlie Munger, Warren Buffett's business partner and the vice chairman of Berkshire Hathaway, said, "Rapid destruction of your ideas when the time is right is one of the most valuable qualities you can acquire. You must force yourself to consider arguments on the other side."

Loss Aversion: This is the tendency of people to give more weight to loss than to obtaining an equal amount of gain. The scales are tilted. This can blind someone who made a previously subpar investment decision to continue doing what is not working for the sake of not "realizing" a loss and changing strategies when it is clearly necessary. Loss aversion can hinder one's ability to make important decisions in real time (when they are actually called for), leading to inertia taking over as a main investment undercurrent.

This Time Is NOT Different

Information disseminated to the public nowadays often seems to have an ax to grind. Similar to the tobacco companies' advertisements of the fifties and sixties, much of it is purely fabricated (dangerously so) with an appearance of legitimacy and consensus. It's rare to hear simply the facts. Conclusions and talking points are made for all of us to gobble up and use to frame our life perspectives. It's a depressing state of affairs. The only way to avoid this trap is awareness.

Apart from the news having a real effect on how we live out all parts of our daily lives and who we are trying to become, there's another very real issue we face all the time with our clients, and the news cycle is the largest villain. It's *fear*. More specifically, how fear plays out in emotional decision making. As investment genius John Templeton stated,

"The four most expensive words are *It's different this time.*"
Those four words are expensive not only because they hurt our
investment return, but that cost bleeds into our ability to live
the life we want, since that life requires financial resources.

As you've probably surmised, we aren't proponents of
spending a lot of time in the "news." But we have a more clear
warning. When you feel the walls closing in and the news
cycle is especially bad and you know that your investments
are down without even looking ... this is a good time to stop
listening to the talking heads for as long as necessary. It could
be three months, six months, or even a year. Turn off the news
feed and go outside every day for a walk.

Our minds tend to give in to fear; this is our default bias.
The scales are not evenly balanced between fear and logic.
They are in fact heavily tipped toward the former. So
naturally, when bad things happen, we are tempted to ignore
history, which very plainly communicates that yes, bad things
will happen, but over time we will recover. As Shelby Davis,
who started investing at age 38 with $50,000 and turned it into
$900 million by the time of his death, stated, "History
provides a crucial insight regarding market crises: they are
inevitable, painful, and ultimately surmountable." You also
may have heard the coined proverb, "It's not timing the
market; it's time in the market."

Do you remember the West Africa Ebola outbreak in
2014? It was certainly a serious disease. But we literally had
a client liquidate a rather large portfolio over this because
he convinced himself that "it's different this time." (This
person is not a client anymore, and he's probably quite
unhappy, because the years since would have been very
profitable for him.)

More recently, we went through a once-in-a-century
health crisis known as COVID-19. We are happy to report
that we didn't have a single client liquidate their investment
portfolio during what was the quickest market selloff in
history. Was it scary? You bet. I (Joel) recall one of the more

intense client conversations in early March 2020. She was wanting to sell, and I simply told her I would be happy to transfer her to the trade desk if she was so bent on this decision, but that I simply could not assist her in trading short-term relief for long-term regret. She didn't sell, and about eight weeks later she wrote to thank me.

We have a chart that shows all the past "it's-different-this-time" events, and the backdrop is the S&P 500 chart moving higher, albeit in a choppy manner. Sure, there are bad events that lead to some short-term craziness. But people have a way of forgetting what they were worried about eventually, only to find new things to worry about.

If we want to worry so much, let's redirect it and worry about how many good things we put in our hearts, minds, and souls this week. What we put in will come out of us, both in words and in actions. If we protect what we let in, we'll be less likely to allow it to control us by moving us to try and control the things that are uncontrollable, like a pandemic or stock market timing.

Benjamin Graham, the "father of value investing," once said, "The investor's chief problem—and his worst enemy—is likely to be himself. In the end, how your investments behave is much less important than how you behave."

Key No. 8 — Connection

What if we told you there's something as dangerous to your longevity as smoking fifteen cigarettes a day?

What if we told you there's something even *more* dangerous than obesity?

Well, it's true, according to a 2018 wide-ranging study by Cigna, the health insurance giant.[33] What is that terrible *something?*

Loneliness.

All through your years in the workplace, you probably had plenty of company (sometimes more than you wanted, right?!). You joined (or created) an organization and forged professional and personal relationships with those on every side. You couldn't help interacting with others in a never-ending inflow. Maybe you even spent more time with some of those people than you did with your own spouse.

If you were also raising children, you interacted with them, their friends, their friends' parents, their teachers, their coaches, and others in the community. During those decades of life, connections were already pre-structured. You simply plugged into certain micro-communities without even trying.

But now ... you've left the workforce. The children have grown up and moved away. Your tight-knit, long-term connections with all of these people hasn't been lost, but the train keeps moving and you are no longer on board. You're not getting that constant supply of new relationships that, in reality, nurture us all without our knowing it. You wake up in a quiet house and have to face another quiet day.

Maintaining a level of connection with others is now a burden we must take upon ourselves. We can no longer consider it to be automatic. Life's new structure no longer provides the daily opportunities to connect. Instead of passively riding the community train that once moved our connections constantly forward on somewhat pre-determined tracks, we're now in an off-road 4x4. This very different, bumpy vehicle has the ability to take us along new and scenic routes, but we must choose to steer in those directions.

What the Research Shows

Studies have found that loneliness is prevalent among retirees for this very reason. So is anxiety and depression. In 2017 a BYU psychologist, Dr. Julianne Holt-Lunstad, presented new research based upon over 200 studies that included about 4 million people. All this data found that those who consider themselves lonely are 50 percent more likely to die prematurely (before their normal life expectancy) than those who consider themselves to be engaged in healthy relationships. She also found evidence to show that social isolation, loneliness, and even living alone increased the chance of a premature death by at least as much as obesity.

We all know that inhaling chemical-laced smoke into our lungs is awful for our health; this is indisputable. What's not immediately obvious is the severely negative mental *and* physical health effects triggered by a lack of connection to others.

Quality Control

So what combats depression fueled by loneliness? It is in fact not the *quantity* of relationships but the *quality*. The depth of meaningful relationships is what truly matters, not the latitude of your social web. You can be a socialite, constantly showing up at parties and community activities, but if your relationships are superficial, there will be little benefit.

The quality of relationships is something directly in our control. We all need to work toward deeper interactions — starting with our loved ones.

As the two of us work with hundreds of households regarding their financial arrangements, it's amazing how often we hear about conflicts that have nothing to do with money. Husbands and wives are clashing when suddenly they're both at home. The two previous lovebirds who led loosely separate lives during the workweeks are now constantly at odds.

In many cases it started right after the initial "sugar rush" (the first six months or so of retirement). Soon one or even both individuals reverted back to what they knew (getting another job like what they did previously). They did this simply to "get out of the house" and chase the old purposeful connections they felt comfortable with, even though this meant just treading water in their lives.

How sad when a real disconnect between spouses shows up just as the season has arrived when they have the most time, resources, experience, and flexibility. They used to be so close. But they've grown apart slowly, like tectonic plates that separate only millimeters at a time due to "busyness" or some other undertaking earlier in life. As with tectonic plates, the problem is that once the separation occurs and continues its slow but steady momentum, it's not easy to bring them back together.

In fact it takes some atypical occurrence to rejoin the pieces, because each side has so much "weight" built up. This effort is the polar opposite of inertia. If you care about your future with your spouse, it needs to be nurtured over time like anything else. This can be beautiful and fulfilling work. And the post-career years can be a remarkable time to revisit this and see where love continues to take you. Time — a seemingly endless tunnel ahead when you both were young — now grows shorter as you age. How unfortunate is the outlook of choosing to walk down that tunnel without a soulmate.

You originally chose to go on this journey with someone special. It's time to remember that and give real focus to what is most likely the most important relationship in your life.

We could share multiple stories of client couples who had been married for over forty years and then got divorced in their "golden years." We won't go into the painful details, but the themes were pretty much the same. Whether it was the business owner who cut back significantly, or the stay-at-home grandma who poured herself into helping raise her grandkids while her daughter worked so hard, they both hit a desert, and they needed to feel *alive* again. Remember the old Johnny Lee song that won a Grammy Award, "Looking for Love in All the Wrong Places"? Well, these were cases of looking for *purpose* in all the wrong places. They didn't *not* love their spouse; after all, they'd been married for forty years or more. But now they just didn't fill the hole with the right things.

Creating your purpose as a couple in the golden years isn't easy; if it were, everyone would do it. It takes work. First, you need to know it's going to be an issue (which you now do), but then you have to work at it. If you don't, you'll skip over the right things and move into the easily obtainable wrong things.

You don't need to "feel" alive; you're already alive. Your feelings are not to be trusted. What you need to know is that the urge will come to fill that retirement hole with something novel and different, when in fact you need to surround yourself with meaningful connections and commit to them. Staying connected isn't easy; there will be lots of times where you don't want to connect. That's normal, but keep doing it anyway.

> **Creating your purpose as a couple in the golden years isn't easy; if it were, everyone would do it. It takes work.**

Are you noticing a pattern here? If *journaling* is your counselor (Key No. 4), and *movement* is your physical therapy (Key No. 3), *connection* is your safety net. The number-one push to move in the wrong direction in life relationships begins with isolation. Each example we could describe had one person who withdrew and began escaping, leaving friends, church, and so forth. One even went so far as to leave the state and never return. Isolation is your enemy.

Other Relationships

Which connections in your life have you neglected during your "busy" years? Which "close friends" have you actually not seen for a long time, even though they're just a phone call away? What relatives have you always wished to get to know better if your schedule wasn't so packed with X, Y, and Z?

Now is the time to ponder the quality of those relationships and start making an effort. If you focus on cultivating better relationships, you'll find you will be less bored, you'll feel more fulfilled, and you'll have outlets to share the deeper emotions that everybody is feeling at any given stage in life but doesn't really talk about because it can be "personal." It's the ignored iceberg mass beneath the surface.

Connecting With Others Through Serving

As we have mentioned previously, this life stage is unique in that you are at a maximal point of experience, coupled with the most time and presumably the most financial resources you have ever had. This potent combination equates to an enormous level of flexibility and the power to be impactful.

Think of your connections with other individuals, families, or organizations. Is there a specific way you can leverage your unique abilities and resources to make an impact? Perhaps it's becoming a mentor-figure, or channeling your specific knowledge from your career in a new way to transform an organization and deepen your connection to the community or people they serve.

Don't underestimate the accumulation of power within you to serve something much larger than yourself. In physics we learn about *potential energy* (imagine a ball being held above the ground) and *kinetic energy* (the ball flying through the air, an energy of motion). Every one of us has a vast amount of potential energy waiting to be used across a needy world. We just need to turn that potential energy into kinetic energy — and we can do that almost exclusively through our connection with others.

It certainly beats squandering our days on social media and web-surfing. Reading anything on the internet in an "online community" does not equate to a meaningful connection. In fact, some current research attributes loneliness to social media and time spent staring at a screen.

> " Reading anything on the internet in an "online community" does not equate to a meaningful connection.

Everybody posts only the best snapshots of their lives to meet that unquenchable societal standard of "perfect." It is a self-defeating cycle, like materialism, where "it's never enough" or "I'm never good enough." That kind of self-talk eventually punctures our self-worth.

Instead, get out and connect with real people. Spend more time with family and friends. Experience life with those close to you. Examine and share all the hardships and trials as well as the successes. In that way you can cultivate your companionship at this critical stage of life. Through those connections you can accomplish great things together, with others.

The African proverb says it well: "If you want to go fast, go alone. If you want to go far, go together."

Key No. 9 — Generosity

If you're no longer working for pay, the idea of generosity can seem odd. Many retirees think, "I've squirreled away this money for the winter—it's all I have. I can't be giving it to something else."

The reaction is entirely understandable. In a season of life where you still have expenses, and a large portion of your livelihood comes from what you've saved, it can be scary.

So the point of this chapter is not to make you "philanthropic." That's a term for rich people who donate so they can be recognized. Actually, your generosity isn't needed in order to save the world or even a worthy local organization. It goes deeper than that.

As in so many areas already discussed in this book, we all have a choice to make. We can choose conventional wisdom and use this season of our lives to be "all about us." We can pack as much away as possible and hope it lasts the winter ... we can fill our barns to the brim and hope it's enough ... in essence, we can rely on ourselves.

Or we can choose something that's bigger than us. This will entail going up against the worldly force of *fear*, which seems to be the dominant binding agent for those trapped. It's the tendency we need to shatter in order to have a breakout moment in our lives — where we step beyond our present and into that new future we've longed for but could never grasp. It's the moment when we put a stake in the ground and choose not to be bound by the forces of this world any longer.

Few practices can turn the fear of your life upside down like generosity. In this chapter we'll talk about being generous with three different resources in your life: money (obviously), time, and a less known form at the end.

Anything but My Money

Money is funny — it makes us act weird. As financial advisors, of course we understand that you need money. Managing money for people is how we make our living, so we're not against it.

But let's talk instead about your *relationship* with your money. If you can manage to view your money as a blessing and a means to facilitate your life's impact, then you're on the right track. However, if you find yourself idolizing your "Benjamins" … if you check your investments daily (or perhaps multiple times a day) in order to gauge how you should "feel," you're falling into a common trap.

> Few practices can turn
> the fear of your life
> upside down like generosity.

If the value of your money steers how you feel, it will certainly impact your close relationships. And if it impacts your close relationships, it will steal your joy. And if it steals your joy, then what's the point of having money in the first place? After all, we can't take anything with us when we leave this world, right?

Many clients over the years have thanked us for helping them get their mind off their money and onto their future.

By the way, you're not weird for fixating on your money. It's absolutely a natural human behavior. In fact, you're not weird for feeling like you want to fixate on your money even as you're trying not to. Let's face it, none of our lives are as perfect as we may portray. So if you're telling yourself, "I know I shouldn't fixate on my money, but I hear things aren't going well in the stock market, and I really want to check to see how I'm doing today," that's *normal*.

What this book is about is understanding that these forces exist and gearing up to combat them, so you can stop succumbing to things that add zero value to your life and lean into the things that will drive true fulfillment.

Financial generosity may be the single most powerful catalyst in changing your relationship with the material realm. It is the polar opposite of spending, greed, hoarding, and material attachment. Whatever you give, whether a $10 bill or 30 percent of your assets, is a resource you are *releasing*. You're intentionally letting go of instant gratification and ownership for the sake of someone else.

The primary force for good in generosity with money is this breaking of control. It's a literal action of trust. It's the antithesis of fear. Generosity is a physical act of giving the one thing you don't want to give.

And what's counterintuitive about financial generosity is that you're the one who actually wins. By doing this, you are surrendering the mindset that you have *control* over your money, how it performs, or what it provides. You have moved from control and fear into *trust*.

Many people would say, "I'll give my time, but don't touch my money." And again, we can't blame them for this viewpoint. But generosity is the gateway to release the desire to control. As the ancient saying goes, "For where your treasure is, there your heart will be also."[34]

At a recent conference we heard a psychologist say that after decades of counseling work, he's learned one truth about each patient's issue: *They were all victims of trying to control things outside their control.* Wow. We both had to plead guilty to doing this. We want to control things just like you do. There is no better way to exit the perceived (but not real) control in your life than to give away some of what is most dear to you.

You may have started this chapter expecting to hear all the ways your money will help others. This is true, of course; you can absolutely make a major impact, which is great news because the world needs more help. However, by being generous *you* break out of the mold, *you* become more effective, and thus *you* live with increased impact and passion. It's *you* that gets better.

Getting Personal

Much like a physical trainer needs to eat well and be healthy, we advisors also need to practice what we preach. (It would be odd if you showed up at the gym on January 2 only to realize your trainer was more out of shape than you were!) Here are two ongoing practices that we both implement in our own personal lives to stay "in shape" so we can "train" clients well.

First, we never check our own investments when we want to, only when we need to (for instance, when we document our personal annual summaries, need to perform some account maintenance such as a rebalance, or perhaps need to provide financial documentation). Now of course we know where our money resides, and we will make a change at any time if necessary. But in general, whenever we have the urge to log in and see what the numbers are, we deny ourselves.

You might say, "I thought I was supposed to check it often. This is what I've always been told." Again, conventional wisdom is often wrong. The more you check it, the more it will own you. (We should mention a caveat here: This assumes you are working with a high-quality and trusted advisor. If so, then you're free to abstain from constant checking. You've implemented a good overall strategy, and so you can sit back and let it work while you place your focus elsewhere.)

What does this frequency of checking your investments have to do with generosity? Glad you asked. The less your investments *own* you, the more generous you can become. It's a self-lifting cycle (not a self-defeating cycle). You are imprisoned less, and thus you become more generous with your resources.

The second practice is that we give financially on a regular basis. It's the primary metric we both track each year. In our minds this comes first, before any other financial objective such as savings goals. We're not saying this to get a pat on the back! In fact, in some ways giving can be "selfish" because by being generous, the giver generally receives the lion's share of the benefit. Does that make sense? The giver is the one who gets to escape the confines of prison where money and control can trap you.

Please understand that you don't need to do exactly what either of us do, or what anyone else does. One physical trainer may have different ideas than the next physical trainer. But the common denominator is that they're both healthy, even if they arrived at that state in a different way. What we're hoping you get from this is that letting go of your control can be achieved primarily through generosity, and the more you let go, the more you'll find yourself pursuing the right things.

Robert Morris is a successful author and Dallas pastor who doesn't hesitate to talk with his large congregation (Gateway Church) about these things, using this imagery: The good life (he calls it "the blessed life") walks on two legs. One is *generosity*; the other is *stewardship*. If you're generous without being a good steward of your resources, you're going to be hobbling all over the place. But if your focus is on stewardship without generosity, you'll be "tight" — a hoarder who never loosens up the purse strings. It's better to walk on both legs.

He tells about standing in line at the counter of a gas station/convenience store waiting to pay for a soft drink, while a middle-aged woman in front of him carefully counted out her coins. In a minute he realized she was scraping up every nickel and penny she had to buy $1.32 worth of gas for her car. That was all she could afford.

She wasn't begging anyone for help. She wasn't holding up a cardboard sign. She was truly just trying to get down the road a little farther.

Robert Morris paid for his soda and then followed her out to the pump. "Excuse me, ma'am," he said, pulling out his credit card, "but I want to buy the rest of your tank of gas." Her eyes flew open in amazement.

Once the gas was pumped, he then pulled a $100 bill out of his wallet (which he had reserved for just these kinds of moments) and said he wanted to give it her — "but I want to tell you why." He recounted a bit of his own personal story, and then concluded, "I'm giving you this money today to remind you that God loves you and has a good plan for your life."

The woman, with tears streaming down her face, hugged him and whispered in his ear, "You'll never know how much I needed to hear this today."[35]

Now we see the shape of a healthy, blessed life. It's managing your resources responsibly (stewardship) so that you have enough to take care of yourself plus extra to be generous toward someone else in need when the opportunity presents itself.

Playing the Long Game

We look at retirement, or the last third of your life, or whatever you want to call it, as a Long Game. Short Games and Long Games have different tenets. At the moment as we write this book, investors have experienced a pretty good increase in their accounts (despite some massive bouts of volatility!). If there were ever a time to think, *I don't know what these two guys are writing about, I'm really enjoying myself and I don't do any of this stuff,* now would be the time. It's a lot easier to neglect the disciplines (journaling, movement, connection, generosity, etc.) when one's net worth is feeling flush and "growth" of investment balances is beginning to feel status quo.

But what about famine? Think of any bull market as a high. The markets are good, and you've been rewarded for making good choices … great, we're all for that. But do know that things will turn sooner or later. The high will wear off, and if you are left with no discipline, then you will find yourself on very thin ice.

We're not preaching doom here. We believe that over a long period of time, if your financial plan is well designed, you'll be just fine. But having said that, will you be prepared for the intense seasons of famine if you didn't invest in yourself or practice important disciplines during the feast? We can answer that one for you because we've seen it happen: The answer is no.

So let's flip the script here and say this: *It's not that you can't afford to be generous, it's that you can't afford not to be.* Here's a very broad generalization: If your financial plan wasn't going to succeed with 90 percent of your assets, then it likely won't succeed with 100 percent. Conversely, if your financial plan was going to succeed with 100 percent, then it will likely succeed with 90 percent. The margin of error isn't that slim.

> " It's not that you can't afford to be generous. It's that you can't afford not to be.

This observation isn't meant to suggest that there's a set definition of generosity equaling 10 percent; it's simply an illustration. As advisors we build very few plans that are meant to let your final check bounce! It's too hard to thread that needle; we need some room to work. Conversely, we've had more than one client look at a prospective plan and react, "Geez, I don't want to leave all that to my heirs; we should spend more now …" but then even with this knowledge, they think they can't "afford" to give much.

This is evidence that generosity is a state of mind, not an action that's dependent on whether or not you can "afford" it. If you think you should wait to give until you think you can afford it, you'll never give at all. So if your plan is mapped out well, generosity will not torpedo it. Give on.

The truth is that we all can give, whether we have a lot or a little. It's not about the amount given, it's about how loosely you hold what's yours. Trust can do tremendous things for you. If you can't bring yourself to be generous, then you're setting yourself up for some serious heartache when times go bad. If you find yourself holding your money tightly, then volatility in retirement will be too much for you to handle. By being generous in both good times and bad, you'll be saying, "It's going to be okay … don't get too excited and don't get too depressed … steady as she goes … I trust the work that's been done … I trust that it's better for me to risk generosity versus clinging to control."

To play the Long Game, we all need our disciplines regardless of how we feel or how our investments are performing at any given moment. We pledge to continue the endless journey of releasing a little more of our perceived control through generosity.

A Lasting Legacy

We all have a choice in what we do with our financial resources while we are alive. We can ask ourselves, "What do I stand for?" and "What do I want the world to look like?" Then we can give to organizations or individuals who are pursuing the paths we value. Supporting your own unique vision of a better world, society, and life for someone else can be deeply fulfilling. It's a living legacy that you can start well before you actually pass on a "legacy" in the traditional sense upon your death. While you have breath, you are breathing new life into the world, and you get to be a witness to that contribution and ultimately its impact.

A living legacy is a remarkable thing. It's the difference between a well-to-do grandparent saying, "One day I'm going to leave this amount of money in my will, or in a trust to each of my grandchildren" versus "I'm paying for the grandkids' schooling now" or "I'm going to do X, Y, or Z now for them and be present in their lives in a specific, ongoing way." The world doesn't need your generosity at your death; that's the easy way out. At death, if you are worth anything above zero, that wealth will go to someone else. It's inevitable. So waiting for your demise to finally let loose of your accumulated wealth is just pure inertia.

The potential for you to make a serious impact starts with cultivating a "today mentality." Doing so results in being able to see your investment in others come to life. What may have started as a tiny dream or utopian vision can blossom into something momentous—and you can be there to see the bloom! The time is now for your effort and generosity, not later.

The old saying "You can't take it with you" rings true, and chances are that whoever receives your financial wealth once you pass will not share the exact passion, ideals, and world vision that you do. Thus the impact ability of your wealth will be diminished if it's all just bequeathed in the future after you're gone, rather than being put to use now.

Clearly, we aren't against leaving assets and wealth to family heirs or beneficiaries. We help clients every day with their estate planning decisions, and in fact we enjoy the work. Everybody's wishes are uniquely their own. But the matter of *when* you leave your legacy is worthy of your deep consideration.

Generosity and Your Time

We find it interesting that people treat their money as more valuable than their time, even though we all know

..uitively that our time is our most valuable resource. Why is that? Because we can't get more of it. It's limited. You can make more money, but you don't get to make more time.

Having a generous mindset is a posture that comes in multiple forms, much like water is a liquid, a solid if frozen, or a gas if it's turned into steam. Being generous is a mindset that can manifest in different ways. All are equally valuable, but each has a different contribution to your life. Whereas giving of your finances can free you from being bound to your wealth, serving with your time keeps you closely connected to the world in a humble way.

The two of us have both served at a no-cost grocery store here in Colorado Springs called Crossfire Ministries. It's funny how before we head down there each time, we feel like we should cancel because we have more immediate things to do. But we've noticed that the longer time passes without our being plugged in, we tend to drift from the benefit of what we experienced the last time we worked there. A little voice inside our heads says, "Oh, you don't need to go do that. You have better things to do. You'll just be wasting your time...."

We've learned from staying disciplined (meaning we keep serving even when we don't want to) that the voice will ultimately be proven wrong, again and again. So we go. Every time, without fail, we drive out of the parking lot saying, "Wow, we can't believe what others are dealing with." It makes us more thankful for what we have.

If the benefit of giving money is that you become more trusting, the benefit of serving is humility—one of the greatest single qualities in a human. It's really easy to drift away from humility when we run only in the circles we're accustomed to. Sure, it's great to go help some poor people, but to be honest, if we didn't show up, the jobs would still have gotten done. So our service wasn't our gift to Crossfire, it was Crossfire's gift to us. We get to spend the next few days with a renewed perspective, and we are able to better serve our families, our clients, and those we rub elbows with daily. We are simply more effective and better leaders because our outlook was readjusted.

It never fails that every time we do this, we are reminded of what's most important. We've never left Crossfire thinking about how our investment portfolios did today, or how we were wronged by So-and-so. You won't find us complaining about things we shouldn't complain about (not for a few days at least). It's impossible to see a hungry child with his mom, or loading a Thanksgiving box for a family that can't afford it, and keep your focus on yourself.

Dean Merrill, our collaborator on this book, is now in his mid-seventies. He spends every Wednesday morning volunteering in an ESL (English as a Second Language) class for newcomers to America. He's not a professional educator (he's a journalist), but he assists the lead teacher in helping young Afghan moms whose husbands had aided the U.S. military, single guys fleeing the hopelessness of Eritrea, and war refugees from eastern Congo. Together they figure out the quirky language they must master in order to survive in this new country. (So why does the verb *to cook* have a past tense of *cooked,* but the past tense of *go* is not *"goed"?* Go figure!) Dean helps set up the room, gets workbooks and pencils ready from the supply closet, helps students with their worksheets, and leads conversation circles where they practice explaining how they came to this country, or what "honesty" means to them. For Dean, it's probably the most invigorating three-and-a-half hours of his week.

This form of generosity is the best way to get your mind off your problems and onto being thankful and humble. This is the tremendous gift of serving others, and it's not to be missed in retirement. Otherwise you'll be tempted to stay isolated, to hoard and not give. Instead, do the opposite!

One More Thing

There's a third, more obscure form of generosity. What is that? It is declining to take what you could have in order that others may benefit. We might refer to this as *selflessness*.

This is incredibly hard, especially when we think we kind of deserve a certain reward. I mean, we've put in the work, perhaps it was our idea—but we choose to lay down our human desires to receive recognition so others can be built up.

A lot of times no one will thank you for this form of generosity, which in turn makes it a very generous gift. The less honor or reward you get for doing something, the more purely generous it was. You don't have to debate whether you served just to get a pat on the back, or if you wrote a check so the organization would honor you. Instead, you can lay your head on the pillow at night and feel good about doing something truly selfless.

> " The less honor or reward you get for doing something, the more purely generous it was.

A great example of this shows up in the ancient story of Nehemiah. He had a cushy job as cupbearer (butler) for the king of Persia, and he wasn't even Persian. Imagine how hard he must have worked to get promoted to this position, being trusted by the king of the most powerful kingdom at the time.

But to make a long story short, Nehemiah couldn't forget that his people back home were struggling. So he left what was comfortable and went to lead them ... selflessly. Nehemiah is most famous for rebuilding the broken wall around the city of Jerusalem. But we would argue it was his humility and generosity that should be magnified.

See, once the wall was up, he knew on the inside that he had been the one who facilitated it. He became the provincial governor. I don't think anyone would blame him for reaping a reward; just look at what he gave up. But Nehemiah used this opportunity to model selflessness. He wrote:

> Moreover, from the time that I was appointed to be their governor in the land of Judah, from the twentieth year to the thirty-second year of Artaxerxes the king, twelve years, **neither I nor my brothers ate the food allowance of the governor.** The former governors who were before me laid heavy burdens on the people and took from them for their daily ration forty shekels of silver. Even their servants lorded it over the people. But I did not do so, because of the fear of God. **I also persevered in the work on this wall, and we acquired no land**, and all my servants were gathered there for the work.
>
> Moreover, there were at my table 150 men, Jews and officials, besides those who came to us from the nations that were around us. Now what was prepared at my expense for each day was one ox and six choice sheep and birds, and every ten days all kinds of wine in abundance. **Yet for all this I did not demand the food allowance of the governor**, because the service was **too heavy on this people**.
>
> Remember for my good, O my God, all that I have done for this people.[36] *(boldface type added)*

Royalty in that era got a rather significant daily stipend of money and choice food from the people. In an unusual act of leadership, Nehemiah refused, saying the all-inclusive cost of providing this would be too great a burden on the populace. He chose not to take what could have been his so that others could benefit. Now that's the type of leader we want to follow.

We talked earlier about everyone being a leader; it's true. But most people who want to be leaders have it backwards. Leadership isn't about getting credit or being the "boss."

Leadership is stepping out of the way of a reward because you care more about others than yourself.

This too is a form of generosity — the generosity of selflessness.

What Is True Generosity?

The benefits of generosity aren't measured by the size of the financial gift, or the time spent pouring yourself into someone or something else. Generosity is an emotional feeling that wells up within you when you give freely; it's a sensation of confidence that you are actively engaged in someone or something other than yourself.

Buying a warm coffee for the school crosswalk volunteer on a frigid day can be just as rewarding as writing a huge check to your favorite nonprofit. The "Giving Pledge" (which Bill Gates and Warren Buffett have gotten many of the world's billionaires to take, promising to donate more than half their wealth to charity while they're still alive) is wonderful. But you and I can receive as much personal growth and fulfillment by giving what we can give to our church or a charity we love. The magic happens not in the magnitude but in the selfless act.

There doesn't need to be some building named after you in order to send ripples across history. Expecting some form of reciprocity does not fully relinquish control; one is still trying to hang onto the power of that donation. Far better to reap the real benefits of openhanded, willing generosity.

Key No. 10 — Awe

Have you ever revisited a childhood home or park from your younger years? In your mind, it was always this enormous and intriguing place. That huge tree in the front yard ... the endless miles of green grass, with limitless possibilities. But when you return as an adult holding those nostalgic pictures in your mind, you're surprised by what awaits you.

Recently I (Alex) went back to see the park of my endless soccer practices and school activities, my piano teacher's house, and our old home with its adventure-filled mountainous backyard rising behind. So many vivid memories. However ... something had changed. The huge backyard where I spent so much time exploring now looked like some scrub oak and rocks on a steep incline. I wasn't thinking now about how much fun it would be to take off into the woods again and build a fort or go rock hunting; instead, I noticed how erosion seemed to be eating into the slope, and how some landscaping would improve things. It certainly didn't seem to be a place of so many epic adventures and excitement I held in my memory and shared in stories with siblings and old childhood friends. In fact, on the surface everything seemed almost laughable in how small and unimpressively normal it all was.

Why was my fond memory of the place so different from the reality I was perceiving?

The only part of the equation that had changed was my own mind. It had narrowed to see the world through an adult's banal viewpoint, entirely missing the blissful awe that we all seem to have in abundance before the world teaches us what we *should* be focused on.

I (Joel) was on the tarmac at LaGuardia airport in New York, heading home from seeing a client. I've flown a lot ever since I was young, when I was first (and have remained) amazed that these massive metal objects could take me to distant places at 30,000 feet. I love seeing the beauty from high above — in this particular instance, the New York City skyline, which never gets old.

But on this day, nearly every person in a window seat seemed to pull out their Sudoku puzzle book or iPhone and lower the window shade! Sitting on the aisle, I'm not the type to speak up and ask them to please raise the shade. But I couldn't avoid shaking my head and wondering how our society has lost its sense of wonder.

Too much of the time, we adults have pulled down the window shades of our lives. We're simply not in awe anymore. How much better off we'd be to leave the shade up for just ten minutes, set our phones down, and gaze at the wider, beautiful world. At what point in our lives did we stop noticing the mind-blowing features of our planet and let them pass us by without a second thought? When did "important" things in life (our daily routine, our checklist of to-do's) supersede all the awe that's constantly in front of us?

The mindset of "I've seen it all before" can feel like a badge of honor, reflecting one's vast experience. But it's that very mindset that causes someone to become stagnant and inactive. The true badge of experience is when you have realized how very little you have actually experienced, and you strive to experience more, do more, and humbly understand more.

> **" ** The mindset of "I've seen it all before" can feel like a badge of honor, reflecting one's vast experience. But it's that very mindset that causes someone to become stagnant and inactive.

Humility is a benefit of widening one's perspective above "myself" and the immediacy of life. When you ponder the beautiful intricacies of everything, it's hard to see value in mundane pursuits that are hollow and unfulfilling. We realize things are much bigger than ourselves.

An Amazing World

The post-career years are a time when finding the awe in your life can connect to pursuing purpose and fulfillment. The idea of "that's old news" leads directly to boredom and unfulfillment, because you cease experiencing the new and become rooted in the familiar. You can become jaded against new experience and amazement.

It doesn't take living in a beautiful or unique place to find awe in life. Roger Penrose, a famous Oxford mathematician and physicist who was a close friend and colleague of the late Stephen Hawking, attempted to prove mathematically how the universe could support life if it had emerged by coincidence. He calculated the probabilities of a universe that would be calm and organized enough to support life, and concluded it was a practical impossibility. "This now tells how precise the Creator's aim must have been, namely to an accuracy of one part in 10 to the 10^{123} power. This is an extraordinary figure. One could not possibly even write the number down in full in the ordinary denary notation..." because it results in a "1" followed by more zeros than there are known individual particles in the entire universe.

On a much smaller scale: Billions of molecules and particles make up our bodies and environment, constantly working in harmony every second as we march through life mostly ignoring it all.

- If you unraveled all of the DNA in your body, it would span 62 billion miles, reaching to Pluto (that's 3.7 billion miles from Earth[37]) and back ... eight times.[38]
- If all the blood vessels in the human body were laid end to end, they would span 60,000 miles, circling the earth more than twice.[39]
- The human nose can detect about 1 trillion smells.[40] And if that isn't astounding, your dog's nose has about 50 times the number of receptors! The part of its brain that's dedicated to smell analysis is about 40 times the size of yours, proportionally speaking.[41]
- Your heart beats about 100,000 times a day, about 2.5 billion times in a lifetime, and over that time it will pump about 1 million barrels of blood, enough to fill three supertankers.[42]
- The earth is spinning at 1,037 miles per hour (creating our 24-hour day) while orbiting the Sun at 66,627 miles per hour. And our solar system itself is in the "Orion Arm" of the Milky Way Galaxy, which is rotating around the center of the galaxy at approximately 448,000 miles per hour. So as you stand still, just know that you are actually traveling at over a half-million miles an hour![43]
- What causes the seasons is only a few degrees shift in the earth's tilt on its axis.
- Light from stars takes so long to travel to our eyes that when you look at the star-speckled night sky, you're actually peering deep into the past. NASA's Hubble Telescope can view galaxies and stars in the universe's

"Deep Field," which is 10-15 billion light years away (or 10-15 billion years in the past).[44]

Are you impressed yet? You should be!

A client of ours is a retired physician, now seventy years old, who understandably spent his entire working life indoors — in clinic exam rooms, intensive-care units, operating theaters, and hospital corridors. He saw the sun and the trees only when he left work at the end of a long day, or went on vacation.

Since then, he's made up for lost time. If we told you how many of Colorado's fifty-eight "fourteeners" (mountains higher than 14,000 feet) he has climbed, you'd be astonished. If we added how many high-altitude races he has run, you'd be amazed. Why does he do it? Hear his explanation:

On a superficial level, climbing summits and doing mountain races provides an immediate feedback of success. You either stand on the summit or you do not. You either go the distance in a race or you do not.

But there is a deeper, more spiritual reason. I never feel more alive or happier than in the mountains. During a climb, my mind becomes released from the usual worries of life and focuses on the immediate concerns of developing a rhythm of effort that can be sustained for hours, of route finding, snow evaluation, and weather conditions. Winter climbs are significantly more demanding and have commensurate elements of suffering and reward. I need to be able to call on multiple skills during a winter climb, including endurance, rock climbing, and ascending ice with crampons and ice tools.

In *all* seasons, the experience of climbing is one of beauty: the early starts under headlamp before dawn graces the horizon, the warmth of the rising sun, following sinuous ridges to graceful summits, wandering through riots of wildflowers during summer, going up snow couloirs [gorges] in spring, looking out at the empty autumn spaces, and enduring the cold and darkness of winter but rewarded by being able to gaze on an endless sea of snow-covered summits. The soul is renewed.

Here is a man who honestly believes the storehouse of awe is not yet even close to being emptied.

Learning to Play (Again)

Every parent remembers how remarkable it was to watch a newborn develop cognitively over the first months, eventually locking their little eyes onto objects. The awe was plainly visible. They were seeing and sensing worldly things as well as emotional feelings for the very first time. No words needed to be spoken to convey how curious and deeply interesting everyday things were to them, like a tree, sunlight, or music.

We can learn so much from children—and this is one of them. Sometimes when young children receive a gift, they unwrap it and choose to play with the box or wrapping more than the actual toy! Meanwhile, we adults are so focused on the endpoint objective that we miss what's going on in the present moment. "Forget the dumb box; look at the toy I just gave you!" we want to say. But the child is caught up in a moment of awe over the box.

Another area historically reserved for children (most certainly not for adults) is *play*. We come home from a long day at work, we're hungry, mentally spent, ready to "relax" — but if we have children or even pets, we walk in the door and all of a sudden, it's *playtime*. The interesting thing about this is that if you allow yourself to get fully immersed in the playtime, you feel rejuvenated afterward. Whether you get down onto the floor with kids, play with their silly toys (so says an adult), sing children's songs, or roll around wrestling with your dog, it all has the same effect. You're letting your mind unlatch from the never-ending barrage of adult responsibilities. You're de-stressing, getting back to basic, simple life. You're removing all the "noise" that life throws at you constantly.

Now this may look different to someone whose children have most likely left the nest. But grandchildren are a perfect opportunity to rekindle play in your life. It removes you from what you "need to get done" in order to do something simply enjoyable. It pulls you from what is expected of an adult of your age, from something to answer the question "What am I accomplishing right now?" You'll find that when you allow yourself to play, you'll naturally smile more, have more energy, and feel more connected to the world and those around you.

Each Breath Is an Opportunity

Gratefulness is an act of being thankful for one's fullness. Our culture is obsessed with telling what you lack, but gratefulness identifies the aspects of your life that fill you up. It's inherently a focus on the most important things in your life. Its very essence is not found in wanting but in gravity, a wholeness of something that you see as being so important that you acknowledge its value in your life.

Like many of the other keys in this book (learning, connection, purpose, movement), awe for us adults takes ongoing practice. We have to intentionally pause our light-speed lives and ponder light-speed itself. Much like the perspective change we experience after attending a funeral or visiting a nursing home, awe can give us a renewed vantage point on our lives, prying open our eyes to truths that lay dormant during the normal ebb and flow of our days.

The island of Santorini, one of the most recognizable places in Greece, has an interesting cultural affinity for awe. It's a crescent moon-shaped island rising hundreds of feet above the ocean's surface, with the inside curve of the crescent being jagged cliffs with whitewashed villages speckling the top edges. Looking out on the Aegean Sea from those cliffs, you can see the still-active volcano that devastated the island in the sixteenth century. The whole landscape is almost surreal.

On the first evening when my wife and I (Alex) were there, we found a quiet cobblestone path with a ledge where we could sit quietly and watch the sunset. As the sky slowly began to erupt in color, we found ourselves surrounded by locals. Restaurant workers, hotel staff, shopkeepers, and other tourists all stopped what they were doing and gravitated toward the cliff's edge to watch the sunset unveil. We realized (after the second night) that watching the sunset as a community is something they value and take seriously. It's a "thing" for them. They actively give it a piece of their lives.

Now, no one would argue that the Santorini sunset should be ignored. But have you ever seen an *uninspiring* or *unimpressive* sunset? Probably not. The country of Greece is one of the most debt-ridden in the world, with ongoing insolvency issues. Their pension system is terribly underfunded, and they grapple with floods of refugees whenever a new issue breaks out in the Middle East or northern Africa, which is often. So it's not like these people don't have things to worry about. But still they pause their lives to soak in the sunset.

It doesn't matter what intrigues you. You simply have to turn down the volume dial of your daily life enough to be able to recognize the inspiration that's waiting for you. As Gandalf, the wise wizard in J. R. R. Tolkien's *Lord of the Rings* saga, said: "All we have to do is to decide what to do with the time that is given to us."

Awe "on the Run"

So why make a place for awe? That's a good question. Awe is rather illusive; it doesn't sit on your calendar ("Be filled with awe at 2:00"). It's not quite as precise a habit as movement, or journaling, or showing up for class at your local university.

Awe pushes beyond "habit" status and into a state of mind. It's a way you live your life. It's the glass through which you see the world.

You may be wondering how you could ever drastically change your life enough to put the *"re"* into *retired*. Seems like a lot, doesn't it? To re-do everything seems too challenging. But awe may be the easiest key of all to use. You just need to remember to take it with you, like your morning coffee.

Awe is also a momentum mindset, meaning, the more you do it, the more you want to do it. It's uplifting. Awe takes your bad day or not-so-ideal situation and puts it into the small perspective where it belongs. Yes, your problems are real, but they are not as big as you think. When we fixate on ourselves, we tend to magnify our issues or our fears. When we fixate on how small we really are, that we're part of something so big and amazing, we find ourselves worrying less about the things we have going on. We benefit greatly from the inspiration we take from our awe. There's less stress, less need for control, less "me-itis."

> Awe takes your bad day or not-so-ideal situation and puts it into the small perspective where it belongs. Yes, your problems are real, but they are not as big as you think.

Awe has another benefit. Even though your days may be somewhat routine, your mindset doesn't need to be. As you drive around running errands or picking up those grandkids, the sky is always different ... the trees are usually a different variety or color ... the mountain may be lit up a different shade of pink ... the sunset may hit the clouds a different way. Routine can have a negative effect on us, making us bored and less inspired. Awe, on the other hand, can be routine's kryptonite in the midst.

It's not just about nature. You can gain a sense of awe from a good story, or watching your family overcome some challenge, or listening to a friend describe one of their awe moments. If you've been around someone who seems upbeat even when their circumstances say maybe they shouldn't be, it's likely they understand awe really well.

I (Joel) was flying back from my son's soccer tournament in Phoenix. Per usual, a stranger was sitting next to me in the window seat. We didn't do more than exchange pleasantries during the flight.

But once we landed, I went to grab my bag in search for a piece of gum. I found it, then closed up my bag. As happens to me from time to time, a still, small voice seemed to pipe up, saying in this case, *Offer him a piece of gum.*

I said back to the voice, *But I've already zipped up my bag. Won't it seem a little weird for him to see me unzip it and offer him some gum he just saw me put away?*

The voice clearly said, *I don't care if it's weird – do it.* In my case, I recognized this as God's nudge. I don't profess to hear it all the time, but I know when I do, because often what he asks of me can be a bit uncomfortable.

So I unzipped the bag again, pulled the gum out, and said, "Would you like a piece?"

Guess what he said? "Yes." (Let the conversation begin.)

"So, is Denver home?"

"No, I'm heading to Kenya today."

"Kenya?"

"Yeah, this is my first time in the United States. I've been here for a week training for my new role."

"Wow, what do you do?"

"I help refugees who are stuck in crisis figure out how to live in the U.S. My organization has a team that lives here. But I'm over on the Kenyan side, and so they like us to understand how it works here so we can better prepare people there before they come."

I have to tell you, in that moment I was in awe. My mind was racing through what this guy deals with in a day – the difference between his reality and mine. As I walked through the airport and drove home, I was unable to shake what a brief exchange had done for my perspective.

I've been practicing awe for a long time. When you do so, it will become more of who you are naturally. So, while noticing the flowers or the sunset is one form of awe, engaging with others' stories is another. Allow others to inspire you; I know this gentleman inspired me. What if I hadn't listened to that voice and offered him some gum? Who would have been the one to miss out? He gained only gum — but I gained awe.

Why Awe Is Good

If you're still not convinced ... here is a list of interesting benefits to awe that have been studied scientifically[45]:

- Diminishes the emphasis on the individual self and our inherent self-interest
- Causes us to become more invested in the greater good and to be more charitable
- Promotes volunteering to help others
- Fosters positive emotions such as joy and gratitude, which are linked to greater health and well-being
- Encourages curiosity and creativity
- Makes us feel smaller, which helps perspective
- Is linked to better physical health. (Awe-prone people show lower levels of a biomarker, IL-6, that reduces their risk of cardiovascular disease, depression, and autoimmune disease.)
- Causes time to expand as we immerse ourselves in the present moment, detached from our normal, mundane concerns
- Sharpens our brains, encouraging critical thinking[46]

Let a sense of awe start to pervade your consciousness, especially here in the post-career years. You're never too old to reap its benefits.

PART THREE

Closing Thoughts

The Power of a Cornerstone Habit

Throughout this book we have mentioned *cornerstone habits.* What we mean by that term is how one of the ten keys we've described can silently improve your life in seemingly unrelated areas without additional effort. Each key is powerful by itself, but so often the benefits of making an effort in one area leads to substantial results in others.

Within a building's foundation, there are different types of supports. For example, the length of a wall is certainly important, but it doesn't help to support adjacent walls. However, the cornerstone serves not only its own function, but also supports many other portions of the overall structure simply by its positioning, with no additional effort.

The key called *movement* is a perfect example of this. If you make the conscious choice to become more active and start exercising, you will begin to notice your body becoming stronger and physical activity becoming less burdensome. Your blood pressure and cholesterol will almost certainly drop, your stress levels and confidence will improve, and so might your interpersonal relationships *(connection).* Even your *awareness* now becomes more readily accessible, and self-speak can become more positive. Exercise may lead you to go outside more, helping you to rediscover *awe* in your life.

Many of the tenets in this book can have this pervasive effect. These cornerstone habits are systemic; one impacts the other.

Where Do You Even Start?

It's not critical that you implement all the chapters immediately to see results in your life. We understand it can seem a bit daunting to get to this point. You may be saying, "Okay, I'm energized to change how I mold my life looking ahead ... but where would I even start?"

It's similar to the feeling you have after listening to a powerful speaker or podcast. You are ready to make changes and tackle the challenges ahead; you sense a new page turning; you feel inspiration welling up within your heart—until you go back to normal life. Within a day or two, the inspiration has seemingly left the building, and you are back to your status quo.

This happens to all of us. It's human nature to see a new way of thinking or action, believe its truth, marvel at what it could do in our own lives ... and then move on without implementing anything.

We acknowledge this. We know we have presented you with a multitude of deep topics to explore. There's no one, correct path to take from here except simply to begin. The ancient Chinese proverb states, "The journey of a thousand miles begins beneath one's feet."[47] All you need to do is progress from where you are now. Take the first step, followed by a second and a third. A downpour of rain doesn't change a granite block, but the slow drip over time does. Water, one of the softest substances, reshapes solid stone gradually through repetitious action. Single droplets impacting an extremely hard, stubborn surface eventually create noticeable change.

We human beings are more like hard stone, set in our ways, and skewed against change. It's in our very nature. As the saying goes, we are "creatures of habit." Any consistent effort we cultivate within ourselves may seem like a meaningless drip in the beginning, but slowly and surely, true change does occur. Eventually we will have been reshaped.

A mistake we've noticed over the years as we've attended seminars or leadership training is the desire to change *everything*. It's classic "paralysis by analysis." By wanting to change everything, we changed nothing—the task was too involved and too daunting.

One of our team members frequently runs our local Pikes Peak Ascent, which is a half-marathon straight up one of the largest mountains in the Rockies, at elevations that feel like someone stole your oxygen. Gina remarked in a recent meeting that in order to attempt such a feat, you *don't* look up at the destination (the summit). If you do, you'll talk yourself out of attempting the challenge, or at least you will rationalize why you won't do as well as you hoped. By focusing on the next step only, not thinking about what lies ahead, you will eventually take yourself farther than you ever thought to be realistic.

Many of the concepts require intentional focus as a starting point. You need to make the investment of pausing your daily life in order to explore the ideas. One does not just press a "Go" button to begin pursuing purpose in their life, or enacting true generosity. These ideas are deeply rooted and therefore require deep reflection to get beneath the surface, down to where fulfillment is waiting.

As we have mentioned throughout this text, none of what we discuss is meant to be a box to be checked and moved on from. Each theme is infinite in your life. The goal is to progress toward the light in the distance, to continue to improve and become stronger, better, more purposeful. There is no end-game, no point in time where one masters *purpose,* or *faith,* or *learning.* All of these hugely impactful areas are a process in and of themselves. It's a cultivation.

A farmer doesn't sow seeds one season and then just sit back for years and reap the rewards. It takes constant effort.

Consider the fact that most likely anything meaningful in your life — family, your children, the relationship with your spouse, your connection to the community, even your professional calling in life — they all have a sort of ongoing permanence. You don't say, "Okay, I told my spouse I love him/her. That box is checked this month, and I'm moving on!"

The consistency of investing in yourself is what will bring rewards in your life. Keep in mind that constant cultivation can seem challenging at first. Being steadfast in your desire to stay consistent in, say, writing journal entries, or being generous, or strengthening connections with people can feel like "work." It can appear at first glance to be draining your energy, but eventually that dynamic changes. You come to realize just how much you need these outlets and undertakings.

Which Road to Travel?

Taking the time and making the effort is certainly not the easiest path. And that is why the latter third of one's life can be a real challenge, and is secretly a disappointment for many. Many choose the well-trodden path, but that bears little fruit. Is the retirement they envisioned all throughout their careers just a mirage? They were told they could just sit back and make retirement a time all about themselves, cushioning their lives on every level now that they have squirreled away enough acorns to avoid doing anything they don't want to do.

Robert Frost's classic poem "The Road Not Taken" ends with this punchline:

> I shall be telling this with a sigh
> Somewhere ages and ages hence:
> Two roads diverged in a wood, and I—
> I took the one less traveled by,
> And that has made all the difference.

So what should you do? You want to begin investing now in your life after work, not just quantitatively but qualitatively. In other words, you certainly need to invest wisely and implement strategies for your financial future, but you also realize that money won't produce happiness in your coming years (it only produces the option of *not* having to do something).

As the wise philosopher Dave Matthews coined in his song "You Might Die Trying," "To change the world, it starts with one step.... However small, the first step is hardest of all." Our suggestion is to pick one thing and start. Be mindful that as you pursue it, it will cascade into other habits and areas within this book. Accept the natural evolution of what pursuing right things will do, which is the production of other right things. One begets another. Don't be overwhelmed with all the changes. Just start somewhere. Pick a cornerstone habit and watch it add support in other important areas of your life.

What a Cornerstone Habit *Isn't*

The earth rotates once every twenty-four hours. We're moving and we don't even know it. Stop for a second and try to feel it. The only evidence of this movement are seeing the stars gradually shift their location in the night sky, and the sun's rising and setting.

The ways in which you choose to spend your post-career time, otherwise referred to as "habits," are doing the same thing to you. Whether you choose one of the ten keys in this book, thereby moving you closer to whom you wish to become, or you choose other habits that move you further away, you are on the move.

In the rest of this chapter, we're going to cover three common habits among retirees that are *not* supportive. They're certainly not cornerstone habits; in fact, they're just the opposite.

This isn't meant to beat anyone up or pile on to something you already know you should address. It's more designed to point out how important it is to be aware of how you allocate your time. If you aren't aware, you can find yourself moving rapidly in the wrong direction.

1. The first is the habit of *self-seeking*. This takes many forms, but is most recognizable within today's social-media culture. People create content designed to reinforce their need to be appreciated or valued. When you see someone's post that has no real meaning other than garnering positive feedback for its author, you're witnessing self-seeking.

Some interesting studies have been done on how social media is an addiction, and it was originally designed with that exact intent. In fact, Sean Parker, the founding president of Facebook, admitted as much during an interview in 2017:

> The thought process that went into building ... Facebook ... was all about: "How do we consume as much of your time and conscious attention as possible?" And that means that we need to sort of give you a little dopamine hit every once in a while, because someone liked or commented on a photo or a post or whatever. And that's going to get you to contribute more content, and that's going to get you ... more likes and comments. It's a social-validation feedback loop.[48]

Did you catch that? When you get a like or a comment, your brain literally produces dopamine. It's the same thing when your text message app dings, and you literally drop everything to go see what it is. This same force keeps us from being able to go anywhere or do much of anything without a phone. We're addicted.

Self-seeking can come in many forms, and we're all guilty. Oh, the lengths to which people will go in order to obtain a small piece of confidence-building approval!

We must not allow our value to rest on positive feedback, especially if the feedback isn't rooted in truth to begin with. These efforts are building only a façade. When we do things designed to make us feel better about ourselves through self-seeking, we are reinforcing bad habits. Whereas a cornerstone habit reinforces good things, self-seeking does the opposite.

You can't build any true meaning and fulfillment on a façade. If you try, you're building on sand rather than rock. The not-so-funny reality is that people may give you the positive feedback you're seeking—but they may not even agree with whatever they are loosely condoning. They could simply be conforming to social norms or "being nice." Meanwhile, you think you received what you wanted, but it wasn't real.

All great deceptions feel good. If they didn't feel good they wouldn't be great. They need to feel good (think dopamine hit) in order to expand and take ground in our lives. But just because it feels good doesn't make it actually good.

> **We must not allow our value to rest on positive feedback, especially if the feedback isn't rooted in truth to begin with. These efforts are building only a façade.**

You may be saying, "Well, I don't have an issue with social media like other people do." Perhaps you don't. But the problem of self-seeking isn't limited to the online culture. It's everywhere around us: how we dress, what we drive, where we live, what club we belong to. Again, none of these things are necessarily bad, unless they become a replacement for our purpose.

Now is a good time to analyze areas in which you may be spending your energy that are moving you *away* from the direction you're hoping to head.

As C. S. Lewis eloquently stated:

We all want progress. But progress means getting nearer to the place where you want to be. And if you have taken a wrong turning, then to go forward does not get you any nearer. If you are on the wrong road, progress means doing an about-turn and walking back to the right road; in that case, the man who turns back soonest is the most progressive.[49]

2. The second bad habit is *judgment.* You probably know someone your age whose every conversation revolves around how other people (the younger generation, the mayor, the governor, the president) are misguided, uninformed, and clueless! When it's over, you feel like heading for a good shower. If you ever need intel on anyone, you know exactly where to go, right?

The habit of *judgment* most often manifests itself as gossip. Judgment is another habit we're all guilty of; no get-out-of-jail-free cards here, and while you're passing "Go," don't collect $200. It's just that some people are much more tenured in it than others.

Judgment is destructive because you project who you hope to be on other people and hold them to a standard that you don't hold yourself to. It takes the focus off what you should be working on and displaces it with a false sense of superiority. If this world can get you thinking and perhaps even believing that you've "arrived" and have it all "dialed in," then it has you right where it wants you — judging others from your own hole you've dug, not the ivory tower you think you stand on.

Be far more concerned about addressing your shortcomings than pointing out everyone else's. This holds true whether it's directed at a friend of a family member or someone more distant, like a political or business leader. How many interactions have you been in that began with how great or how poor some leader was. The truth is, we've never been in that person's role and probably never will be. It's safe to assume the role is harder than we think. When in doubt, play the grace card first.

3. The third harmful habit for retirees is *excess.* Even good things can become bad if there's an overabundance. This was originated by Shakespeare about four centuries ago as he coined the phrase "too much of a good thing."

This one is rather camouflaged. We witness people entering retirement with a sense of excess toward certain things they lacked during their working years. To use an obvious example, take travel. Of course we all relish the idea of travel. No problem there. It's wonderful to explore new places and learn.

But consider this: Let's say you have five critical plants that are a combination of things you desire. You've also been given just enough water to maintain all five well. You happen to value the fifth plant over the other four because its blooms are colorfully exotic. The more you water it, the quicker it grows … for a time.

> ❝❝ Even good things can become bad if there's an overabundance.

And then, eventually the plant is full grown. The excitement of enjoying its beauty passes. You pivot back to the others — but they're no longer viable. They've been neglected, and you don't have enough water left. You can't grow the other four by watering the fifth.

Now let's translate this to a real-life example. It begins with a trip to that place you always wanted to go, and it was everything you thought it could be. What's next? You start planning the next trip, but this time there will be two stops, for an even more amazing time. What's next? The third trip, coupled with tremendous amounts of planning effort, goes longer and farther. It turns out great, but not entirely what you had hoped for. So now maybe you could go all the way around the world; that would be the ticket!

We have asked many clients over the years after they return from a travel bonanza, "So how was it?"

Surprisingly, the reply more than often has been, "It was good, but we were ready to get home. Probably won't do that again."

Also, it gets really expensive to one-up your last trip every time. Not many retirement budgets can sustain that. In no way does this make travel bad. It simply illustrates that too much of one thing steals other things from you, while the lure of the plant you were watering so heavily wears dim. The antidote to excess is balance.

Certainly there are more habits to avoid than these three, but we need to stop here. The more we write about habits to avoid, the more convicted we become that our own objectives are not in perfect alignment! In fact, they never will be.

If you were to set this book down, cast off the negative habits as much as possible, and use the ten keys more evenly, you'd be taking the most important step in the retirement process. Knowing what the objective is, even if it's not played out perfectly, is far ahead of not knowing who your enemy will be one day until it's too late.

It was one of the most unique moments we've had in a financial plan meeting. Jim and Lois were about a year out from retirement and planning to move south of the border. We proceeded, as we do with all our planning clients, to forecast their monetary future. The program we use has a blue line that denotes the year of retirement, which largely signifies when a person's primary source of income ends and their self-funding years begin. Sure, it's a little scary, but mostly exciting.

Jim fixed his eyes, however, on the second line, which was gray. "What's that?" he wanted to know.

We responded with "That's your death," thinking we'd get a quick laugh and move on, as often happens. But Jim got very quiet. We found out later that this had stunned him; it was as if he'd just been told, "You're going to die."

When you look at a single sheet of paper that lists the dates from your retirement to your death from top to bottom, things get really real. Back when you were younger, you could afford to be aimless because you had time on your side. You could say, "I'll figure it out later." But as time shrinks and purpose becomes more elusive, you can quickly get depressed if you enter with the wrong posture and mindset. This stage of life can't be about just "holding on," because you have to admit that try as you may, you can't win that battle. Instead, you have to focus on finishing strong with whatever time you have left. Each day has to be maximized.

No Time to "Lose"

Actually, we've noticed that when people think about their last season of life, they largely discount the last ten years as a lost cause. They imagine they'll be battling health and gravity, confined to their home, or worse yet, a nursing home. But in the interim, they want to push retirement age further out, waiting until age seventy to start Social Security while socking away a little more money for what could be twenty to twenty-five years of no earned income and lots of "to-do's." They envision their next ten to fifteen years as their sweet spot, where they believe they'll have good health and capital and can make all kinds of good things happen.

When you come face to face with the reality that your "gray line" is uncomfortably close to your blue line, it's sobering. It's as if we all know we're going to die one day, but we simply don't believe it. We prefer to live our days like there's an endless supply of days yet to come. Sure, we've all heard the phrase "Live today like it's your last," but in all honesty, this has no effect on us. After all, we have too many things that society has convinced us to worry about ... too many things we *need* to do today. We can't afford to actually live like that, right? So, we want to do a lot to make the next two decades a fairy tale!

If so, it's worth going back to the beginning of this book and starting over. Let us restate that there's nothing worse we see and hear than a couple thinking that the main point of the next ten to fifteen years is filling the old bucket list. Not because those items are bad, but because we know that when not properly balanced with all the other things we've discussed, they will return to our offices with the mental anguish of realizing they've almost wasted what little they had left. The bucket list pursuits, in and of themselves, never fill the bucket. This is a desperate place to find yourself— realizing that what you thought you wanted wasn't actually what you wanted.

A New Kind of Bucket List

Rarely is a bucket list loaded with selfless acts of generosity or challenging undertakings that can create lasting fulfillment and personal growth. It's usually filled with special places to visit, relaxing vacations, unique purchases, epic adventures to be had, with perhaps only a spritz of purpose-driving aspects. Travel and adventures aren't poor bucket list items in and of themselves, but one should really consider why they're there. Most of us have utopian ideas of what we would love to do, but if we stop for a second, write the list down, and ponder each one in depth, we might realize that many of our items are somewhat aimless and empty.

> Most of us have utopian ideas of what we would love to do, but if we stop for a second, write the list down, and ponder each one in depth, we might realize that many of our items are somewhat aimless and empty.

At the same time, some might really strike a chord in your heart and soul. So be very intentional about what goes onto your list, and then take steps to see them become reality.

One straightforward way to gauge the depth of meaning of items on your list is to ask yourself a simple question: *If I were given only a year to live, which of the items on my list are actually important to me?* Should seeing the Eiffel Tower or golfing at Pebble Beach even be on the same list as taking the grandkids on a special trip, or teaching them how to fish, or joining a non-profit that works to end modern slavery in Asia? (Some retired clients of ours spend all of their time doing this exact thing.) There are many "wants" in the world, but even more "needs." The needs just aren't as loud and usually don't generate the immediate gratification that a more self-centered bucket list offers.

I (Alex) keep a bucket list of sorts for myself and another one that my wife and I keep for our family as a whole. We adjust and add items over time as we ponder our lives, who we wish to be, and what our future could hold. It's a very insightful process to sit down with a blank page and write out a bulleted list of the fifty things (or whatever number you land on) that you wish to do in your lifetime. It starts out with the low-hanging fruit desires (hike the Pacific Crest Trail, see the Pyramids), but as you reflect, the philosophical, spiritual, and legacy sides enter the exercise, and your inputs completely change. You may even begin to go back to the first few you quickly scribbled down and make changes, as your new more deeply focused lens sees them for what they are (or aren't).

Over time, dreams and needs change, so don't feel weird about upending your bucket list as long as you are being true to yourself. We personally have been fortunate to be able to cross a few items off our list already; we continue to have discussions about what are our true objectives during our brief but glorious time on earth.

> **❝** Over time, dreams and needs change, so don't feel weird about upending your bucket list as long as you are being true to yourself.

So much lasting purpose can be found by evaluating your list of lifetime wants and needs, and then prioritizing what is most dear to your heart, pursuing it while you can.

The bucket list needs to be linked to the ten keys. Even the last decade of one's life does not have to be "lost," as many believe. It is just a different set of circumstances within which to live your purpose.

We understand that when faced with a short time horizon, the temptation is strong to fill the void through indulgence. But friends, you're not needing to see a certain place before you can be happy. You don't need to be on that beach one last week in order to hit your fill. What you need first is to boldly pursue your purpose and allow these other amazing experiences to be your "garnish" as opposed to your sustenance.

If you try to fill your purpose with awesome experiences, you never will. You'll find yourself thinking, *If I just had that mountain home ... or that remote cabin I've wanted ... If we had the budget to travel more ... then I'd find what I'm longing for.* No, you won't. Not only that, but your retirement budget won't like it either! You can't take a trip long enough, you can't relax well enough, you can't ponder on a beach deeply enough. Why? Because we were never made to find our fulfillment in the pursuit of self. It's not how we're hardwired.

Our absolute favorite thing is to watch a friend and client living out a beautiful tapestry of balance between *leaning in* and *living out* – a mix of self-disciplines, meeting others' needs, and taking in new and amazing experiences. It may not look exactly like what you dreamed it would, but this is where the treasure lies.

The world has a way of making the incredibly important seem useless, and the useless seem incredibly important. This is the root premise of the "retirement lie." If we buy this lie, the debt will be too great.

> **The world has a way of making the incredibly important seem useless, and the useless seem incredibly important.**

You are the artist of this picture. It's your job now to bring together the different shades, shapes, and colors. Don't let it all be just orange; you won't be pleased with the result.

What Defines "Amazing"?

It's common for people to falsify their retirement as "amazing" when it's far from it. We've seen it. Why is that?

Two predominant reasons. First, people are more interested in perception than reality. They somehow find contentment in falsehood. If other people think we have it all figured out, then we convince ourselves that we do. This is a coping mechanism many use to get through this challenging life, but it keeps us feeling okay instead of dealing with the underlying illness.

Second, people are embarrassed about their retirement seemingly lagging everyone else's ... so they say theirs is great too. No one wants to be outside the social norm. No one wants to ask, "Hey, what am *I* doing wrong here? Everyone seems to be enjoying it tremendously except me." Pride is so much easier than humility. It takes true humility to be honest when it questions the perception others have of you, doesn't it?

The best way is to make sure your reality and your public profile are equal. If you put the work in on some of these ten keys, your perception will be reality, or at least in much closer proximity.

Whether you're running a half marathon up a mountain or pushing yourself in some other discipline over years and years, it's how you address the challenge that makes all the difference. We know some of the examples we've used along the way seem unattainable to many readers. That's okay; they seem unattainable to us too. But that doesn't mean they're not useful. These lofty goals call us out of our place and move us more toward who we need to become. Being in awe of what others have been able to accomplish helps us close the gap between where we are and where we can move to. The goals may not pull us all the way there, but even a few feet in the right direction makes a difference. Watching others rise to their individual occasions gives us all a sense of what's possible.

Remember, you don't need to be exactly like anyone. Their goals aren't your goals. Some of us are just trying to get out for a daily walk—forget climbing mountains. But if the knowledge of what others were accomplishing gets you out of the house to go on that walk, then that's the point. This isn't a competition. This isn't trying to keep up with the Joneses. This is simply a call to a better version of your current self.

Herein lies your gauge for progress. Use others as motivation to take that step! Whenever I (Joel) am doing something that has pushed me to my limit, whether it's a physical workout or a mental challenge, I reach a point where I want to justify quitting. I can come up with all sorts of excuses. *I didn't sleep well last night. I'm just worn out from taking care of the six kids. Work has been really stressful....* The problem here is that we'll always have some excuse.

So I tell myself this the popular saying, "You can always quit *tomorrow.*" Sometimes I have to take it down to an ever shorter horizon: "You can quit in a few minutes, but not now." It's amazing how many situations this self-talk has pulled me through.

A lot of the secret to activating the ten keys lies in the simple act of not quitting. Press on. Yes it's hard, but that's what makes it good, right? How many things in your life are both fulfilling and easy? We all know the answer to that question.

You will absolutely feel like quitting on these disciplines. This is hard work. But, of what significance is the reward if the challenge isn't great? The good news is that you absolutely *can* pull these off, and you'll enjoy the journey along the way. It's not like you'll be in a miserable slog here. The more you engage, the more you will appreciate the effort required and the results received. Soon you won't know how you did life any other way.

Perfection Isn't the Goal

After leaving the office of the presidency in 1909, Theodore Roosevelt spent a year hunting and adventuring through central Africa. Then he continued his worldwide tour through northern Africa and then across Europe. He stopped along the way giving speeches in storied places such as Cairo, Berlin, and Oxford.

In April 1910 he gave a speech in Paris that became one of his most famous because of this passage:

> It is not the critic who counts; not the man who points out how the strong man stumbles, or where the doer of deeds could have done them better. The credit belongs to the man who is actually in the arena, whose face is marred by dust and sweat and blood; who strives valiantly; who errs, who comes short again and again, because there is no effort without error and shortcoming; but who does actually strive to do the deeds; who knows great enthusiasms, the great devotions; who spends himself in a worthy cause; who at the best knows in the end the triumph of high achievement, and who at the worst, if he fails, at least fails while daring greatly, so that his place shall never be with those cold and timid souls who neither know victory nor defeat.

Roosevelt understood the curious idea of perfection well: it's in the challenge, not the outcome. He was the first American to win the Nobel Peace Prize (1906). He facilitated Panama's independence from Colombia so that our country could purchase and construct the Panama Canal expressly for our trade and military interests. He also prioritized conservation of our natural resources for the first time, setting aside more land for national parks and preserves than all of his predecessors combined, while also creating the U. S. Forest Service and the first national forests. He clearly produced lofty results, but his speech underscores where he saw the value. It wasn't in the accolades and history books, it was in the fight, the "great devotions in a worthy cause."

Do you believe you are in the "arena," or simply watching from the grandstands (or worse yet, the TV)? You have all the tools at your disposal right now, in this very minute, to rise to the challenge and be the one pursuing true fulfillment and a life that truly is worthy of dreams. It's your choice.

Living Terminal

Many of us have known someone diagnosed with a terminal illness. The emotional trials of their journey is daunting to us. All of a sudden their mortality quickly comes to the forefront of their life. Every minute they are reminded of the finality of life and are molded by a change in perspective as they search for meaning while combating some terrible disease or circumstance.

The light is always more noticeable in the darkness. So often a terminal condition can bring immense clarity and perspective to the afflicted person and also the people surrounding them in their journey. Bringing the limits of life to the forefront, the situation begs the questions "What is truly important to me?" and "What do I feel the need to do before I'm gone?"

Isn't it odd that we discover so much useful life perspective only after receiving a terminal diagnosis? We feel a stronger magnetic pull toward the connections that matter most to us in life. We view each day as being vastly important. Most likely we explore faith more deeply, and our focus becomes pinpointed on what is deeply meaningful.

Now, wouldn't it be pure bliss to live this way *without* the specter of sickness and death within sight? How many decades of spectacular living could be had truly celebrating each moment, not simply following society's grind and being caught up in the minutia?

Paul Kalanithi, a thirty-six-year-old Stanford neurosurgeon who was diagnosed with stage IV terminal lung cancer, said this:

> In some ways, having a terminal illness makes you no different from anyone else: Everyone dies. You have to find the balance—neither being overwhelmed by impending death nor completely ignoring it.
>
> It is a struggle. The problem is not simply learning to accept death. Because even if you do come to terms with

finitude, you still wake up each morning and have a whole day to face. Your life keeps going on, whether you are ready for it to or not.[50]

It's challenging to remove ourselves from the strong currents of our lives to find that balance Dr. Kalanithi spoke about. For most of us we are not in an "impending death" scenario, which is exactly why we completely ignore the brevity of life for now. But indeed, we all are terminal, and the precious time we do have is finite for each of us. Accepting this truth and acknowledging that the locomotive of our lives is chugging along every second, we have a choice. Do we reshape our approach to daily living through this perspective and live as though time is of the essence? Or do we continue to ignore our terminal condition, until one day we find we've inadvertently postponed so much in our hearts that is deeply meaningful, mindlessly wasting our precious time on unimportant pursuits. In that moment of realization, we'll have no recourse to do anything about it!

The Dash

Imagine this scene: There we stand, facing a stone on the grass, surrounded by many other stones, with flowers next to each. What's most fascinating about a tombstone isn't the color, the shape, or the size. It's the dash between the two four-digit numbers. We cannot help but wonder, "Did this person have a marvelous journey? Was it a story for the ages? What actions lay between those dates? If they could come back and speak with us, what would they say?

"'I want to play one more round of golf'?

"'If only I could travel to one more place'?

"'Don't push yourself'?

"'As the end nears, do things just for you'?"

Hardly.

They would be encouraging: "You're highly capable, more than you give yourself credit for. You are impactful.

You are unique, and the world needs you. So sprint to the finish. Give it all you've got with all you have left in you. Push yourself every day.

"You don't have to beat anyone; just do *you* to the fullest extent possible. Don't worry about all the stuff you worry about. Don't let the world tell you what's important; instead, you tell it.

"Fight for what's good. Reject selfishness. Put others ahead of you."

In essence, they'll tell you all the things you need to know in order to flip the script. And that's what this book is all about—taking the script that is easily played out and turning it on its head to produce a life worthy of dreams.

What will *your* dash say?

Stand Unashamedly Tall

During our working years and beyond, we face a new crossroads every day, a new decision point that readjusts our life trajectory. Our every thought, action, and interaction are shaping who we are in this moment but also who we will be. Societal gravity is constantly at work, attempting to grind us down over time.

Usually it does not feel like it's coming at us from an exterior source at all. Many of us are strong-willed enough to believe we are following our own path, not doing this or that just for external attention. The problem is that much of the societal pressure we must combat comes from within. It's a subconscious that sprouted within over years and years of being inundated by those sources of influence. And so sometimes our desires and vision of the future are tainted by that unseen pressure even when we are completely unaware of its presence in our life.

So after recognizing this fact, the next step is to set your life in motion in your own way by seeking true meaning and fulfillment. Stones from the mountain roll downhill because it's easy; they let gravity take them where it may. But the mountain itself rises upwards in direct opposition to gravity, pushed by some remarkable force beneath the mountain at its core. The pursuits of purpose, faith, of deepening your connection with others, a hunger for learning, experiencing the new, rekindling a sense of awe in your life, practicing generosity in its many forms, refocusing your awareness, managing your time as the important commodity that it is, being committed to journaling and personal reflection, and maintaining an active lifestyle—all of these in their own unique way combat the strong societal pressures we all face.

The retirement mirage is there, waving at all of us in the fog of our futures, tempting us to sit in a lounge chair on a beach with an umbrella drink, awash in self-aggrandizing comfort. Instead, we must seek the sand below our feet and look beyond the misleading mirage, so we can stand tall as a mountain.

The journey ahead for each of us is filled with uncertainty, emotional zeniths and valleys, obstacles, successes, new relationships and experiences—all while attempting to slow down the endless click of the watch's hand until the battery of our lives runs out. Be gentle with yourself during this season, and realize how much we all must process and persevere in life. It's not easy or comfortable, but it's real. Take the pursuit of purpose and the keys we discuss in the book and integrate them where they will be impactful for you in your life.

We all are in our own little boats, paddling to stay afloat while being flung around by the sea. Remember that there is hope, even if the outlook is stark. If you can find compassion for yourself and constantly strive for meaning, you'll discover that in those stormy clouds ahead is a dove grasping an olive branch, and it has been with you this entire time.

Disclosures

This material represents an assessment of the market environment at a specific point in time and is not intended to be a forecast of future events, or a guarantee of future results. This information should not be relied upon by the reader as research or investment advice regarding any funds or stocks in particular, nor should it be construed as a recommendation to purchase or sell a security. Past performance is no guarantee of future results. Investments will fluctuate and when redeemed may be worth more or less than when originally invested. The S&P 500 Index is an unmanaged index of 500 stocks that is generally representative of the performance of larger companies in the U.S. Please note an investor cannot invest directly in an index.

References

1 Throughout this book's various stories, certain names, places, and other identifiers have been changed to respect privacy. However, the essence of each account is faithful to what occurred.

2 "Retire on Purpose — Beyond Financial Planning: Creating the Life You Want" graphic presentation from Jackson National Life Insurance Company®, copyright 2017

3 "Q&A Dan Buettner," *AARP Bulletin*, Dec. 2019, 36.

4 https://www.pewresearch.org/fact-tank/2017/03/09/led-by-baby-boomers-divorce-rates-climb-for-americas-50-population/

5 https://www.ncbi.nlm.nih.gov/pmc/articles/PMC2442377

6: https://www.census.gov/content/dam/Census/library/publications/2020/demo/p25-1145.pdf

7 Exodus 16:3

8 As quoted by Bob Buford in *Finishing Well: the Adventure of Life Beyond Halftime* (Grand Rapids, Mich.: Zondervan, 2011)

9 Richard Quinn, "Still Learning" (posted at https://humbledollar.com/2019/01/still-learning/)

10 "From Making the Numbers to Teaching the Numbers," *Second Stories — How 10 People Transformed Their Post-Career Lives,* published by Jackson National, 2018, p. 11

11 https://www.nytimes.com/2018/03/30/health/unretirement-work-seniors.html

12 Rob Cowles and Matt Roberts, *The God of New Beginnings* (Nashville: W Publishing Group, 2018) p. 15

13 https://solarsystem.nasa.gov/solar-system/sun/in-depth

14 C. S. Lewis, *Mere Christianity* originally copyrighted 1952 (HarperSanFrancisco, 2001 edition).

15 http://psycnet.apa.org/journals/pag/28/2/578

16 https://www.ncbi.nlm.nih.gov/pmc/articles/PMC3632802

17 https://health.harvard.edu/staying-healthy/exercising-to-relax

18 https://time.com/4336391/sheryl-sandberg-facebook-uc-berkeley-commencement-speech-husband-death

19 https://learning.linkedin.com/blog/top-skills/why-creativity-is-the-most-important-skill-in-the-world

20 Psalm 103:15-16 NLT

21 https://www.nytimes.com/2015/06/28/magazine/confessions-of-a-seduction-addict.html

22 https://www.usatoday.com/story/opinion/voices/2018/09/06/gray-divorce-elderly-couples-marriage-column/1183820002/

23 https://www.usatoday.com/story/opinion/voices/2018/09/06/gray-divorce-elderly-couples-marriage-column/1183820002/

24 Hebrews 11:1 KJV

25 Erwin McManus, *The Last Arrow: Save Nothing for the Next Life* (Colorado Springs: WaterBrook, 2017), 19-21

26 *A Year with C. S. Lewis* (New York: HarperOne, 2003), Sept. 18 reading

27 https://www.cslewis.com/faith-is-a-habit/

28 Romans 12:9-19, 21 ESV

29 "The Impact of Sustained Engagement on Cognitive Function in Older Adults: The Synapse Project" 8-NOV-2013 Co-authors include Linda Drew, Sara Haber, Andrew Hebrank, Gérard N. Bischof, and Whitley Aamodt, all of the University of Texas at Dallas, and Jennifer Lodi-Smith of Canisius College, https://www.ncbi.nlm.nih.gov/pmc/articles/PMC4154531/

30 1 Corinthians 5:6

31 https://newsnetwork.mayoclinic.org/discussion/mayo-mindfulness-overcoming-negative-self-talk/

32 JPMorgan Asset Management "Guide to the Markets" December 31, 2019. Average asset allocation investor return is based on an analysis by Dalbar Inc., which utilizes the net of aggregate mutual fund sales, redemptions and exchanges each month as a measure of investor behavior. Returns are annualized (and total return where applicable) and represent the 20-year period ending 12/31/18 to match Dalbar's most recent analysis.

33 https://www.webmd.com/balance/news/20180504/loneliness-rivals-obesity-smoking-as-health-risk

34 Matthew 6:21

35 For a fuller treatment of this perspective, see Robert Morris's book *Beyond Blessed* (Nashville: FaithWords, 2019).

36 Nehemiah 5:14-19

37 https://solarsystem.nasa.gov/planets/dwarf-planets/pluto/in-depth/

38 http://scienceline.ucsb.edu/getkey.php?key=144

39 https://health.howstuffworks.com/human-body/parts/facts-about-the-human-body.htm

40 https://www.sciencemag.org/news/2014/03/human-nose-can-detect-trillion-smells

41 https://www.pbs.org/wgbh/nova/article/dogs-sense-of-smell/

42 https://www.pbs.org/wgbh/nova/heart/heartfacts.html

43 https://www.space.com/33527-how-fast-is-earth-moving.html

44 http://coolcosmos.ipac.caltech.edu/ask/284-How-far-can-the-Hubble-Space-Telescope-see-

45 https://greatergood.berkeley.edu/topic/awe/definition#why-practice-awe

46 https://www.psychologytoday.com/us/blog/the-athletes-way/201505/the-power-awe-sense-wonder-promotes-loving-kindness

47 Lao Tzu, *Tao Te Ching,* written sometime between the 4th and 6th century B.C.

48 axios.com/sean-parker-unloads-on-facebook-2508036343.html

49 C. S. Lewis, *Mere Christianity* originally copyrighted 1952 (HarperSanFrancisco, 2001 edition), 28.

50 Stanford Medicine, "Scope 10k": "Stop skipping dessert:" A Stanford neurosurgeon and cancer patient discusses facing terminal illness